My
Dinner
of
Herbs

My
Dinner
of
Herbs

EFREM ZIMBALIST, JR.

LIMELIGHT EDITIONS
NEW YORK

First Limelight Edition July 2003
Copyright (c) 2003 by Efrem Zimbalist, Jr.

Published in the United States by
Proscenium Publishers, Inc., New York

Manufactured in the United States of America

LIBRARY OF CONGRESS CATALOGING-IN-PUBLICATION DATA
Zimbalist, Efrem, 1923-
A dinner of herbs / Efrem Zimbalist, Jr.— 1st Limelight ed.
p. cm.
ISBN 0-87910-988-2 (hardcover)
1. Zimbalist, Efrem, 1923- 2. Actors—United States—Biography. I.
Title.
PN2287.Z56A3 2003
791.45'028'092—dc21
2003000424

To my cherished Lu, Skipper, Alexis, McNair, Kristina,
E. Z. IV, Blivet and Squiddel, whose idea this was,
who gathered the material, and rode herd on me.

With heartfelt thanks to Dennis S. Brown
for his invaluable assistance

and a grateful bow to
Christina Boehme and Nina Maynard.

Better is a dinner of herbs where love is,
than a stalled ox and hatred therewith

PROVERBS 15:17

Prologue

WHEN I WAS GROWING UP I WAS AN INVETERATE MOVIEGOER, sometimes sitting through two double features a day. I also devoured *Photoplay* and *Silver Screen*, luxuriating in each and every revealing facet of my favorite stars' lives that the studio publicity departments saw fit to release. That company included Douglas Fairbanks, Errol Flynn, Ronald Colman, Greta Garbo, Gary Cooper, Irene Dunne, George Arliss and a dozen others. They were my heroes and they spoke to me directly, soul to soul, with little or no dependence upon the lines they were reciting or the plot in which they found themselves. If you had asked me what I thought of their acting I would have suspected your brains had escaped through a hole in the skull. The asking would be equivalent to questioning Flynn's swordplay, or Fairbanks's calisthenics. What my people dealt in was beyond acting—it was illusion—and when it was all over I felt exalted, ennobled and at least an inch taller.

Years later when I came to Hollywood myself I had no illusions whatever about my capacity to invest an audience with such wonders as these. Nonetheless I did find myself grateful, through no doing on my part, to be dispensing merchandise from a lower drawer, but not the lowest. I took comfort in reckoning that I was not contributing to a devaluation of morals, nor augmenting those stresses and passions which the news media seemed quite able to inflame unassisted. If I was privileged to provide an hour's surcease from those very tensions—traffic, family squabbles, the depredations of the IRS, politics, financial and job insecurity or unrequited love—it was enough; and whether or not this entailed a shift in loyalty from Thespis to Hippocrates was and is of indifferent consequence to me. Theatre and healing didn't share the same umbilical cord in ancient Greece by accident.

This storybook, casting a fond look through the rearview mirror, is offered in the simple hope that it may bring pleasure and that, unlike the upturned corners of the moon which hold back the hypothetical water from spilling, those of the reader's lips may release, instead, the hint of a smile.

Solvang, California, October 8, 2001.

My
Dinner
of
Herbs

"The Rafters"

One

"THE RAFTERS," MY FAMILY'S SUMMER HOME IN Connecticut, was built by a retired captain in Washington's army. A portrait of him and his wife survives in the living room, along with a legend of dubious authenticity. According to tradition the two, for whatever reason, had not spoken in decades, their sparse intercourse consisting of brief messages left about on scraps of paper. She slept upstairs, he directly beneath her. One day following a particularly rancorous exchange of notes he is reputed to have placed an explosive charge under her, propelling her well on her way to heaven, if that was her destination or, in the other event, causing a considerable delay in her arrival. The only circumstance that lent cogency to the myth and may, indeed, have occasioned it was the fact that no ceiling existed above the living room. Instead, an open space extended all the way up to the ancient timbers supporting the roof, and after which the house came to be named. There was a simple stairway along the southern wall that rose to the level where the ceiling should have been, from which point a balcony took off at right angles and ran the length of the living room, giving onto three bedrooms.

There were no paved roads when we came there, nor was there electricity. After dark one depended on kerosene lamps, and food preservation called for canning, as well as storage in the root cellar. A shed with sawdust packing was replenished a few times a year with great blocks of ice, which were carried into the house by tongs and loaded into the icebox. When I was big enough to manage it that became my "chore," as well as banking the coal-burning furnace before going to bed. This simple, rural existence had enormous appeal for my mother, Alma Gluck, whose former brilliant singing career and

With sister Maria and Mother, 1924

social responsibilities had left her little time to enjoy the harvest of her prodigious labors. As if designed to withstand the corrupting inroads of the twentieth century the old saltbox, surrounded by forty-five acres of woods and fields, was located in a particularly in-accessible part of Connecticut.

In the prodigal years before the great crash of 1929, "The Rafters" was used as a stopover. For two weeks in late spring while my par-ents' New York house was being mothballed and their main summer residence on Fishers Island readied for use, we would bivouac at "The Rafters." The same procedure was followed in the fall, with the role of the houses reversed.

My mother's favorite spot on our property was the "gorge," where she labored contentedly in her rock garden. I've never known her to be happier than at "The Rafters;" she was like a child playing house. She delighted in all the local activities, from the doings at the Grange to the weekly auctions conducted by Fahey and Co., where magnificent early New England pieces could be picked up for a song.

Twice during the summer months my mother, my sister Maria, a few friends and I would hike up the mountain behind "The Raf-ters," blazing a trail through the woods. Near the top we would spread blankets over a huge rock in a clearing, eat our sandwiches and stretch out under the stars to give the mosquitoes their turn. In the morning, eaten alive, we would cook breakfast hastily before fol-lowing our blazes back down to the sanctuary of screen doors and a Flit gun.

My father, who welcomed "The Rafters" as a haven from the rig-ors of his concertizing career, was less than happy there in the first years. The mosquitoes drove him crazy, his thin fair skin being ex-traordinarily sensitive to their ravages. Twice he fled—once with Maria to Fishers, where he had bought a piece of property at the "club" end of the island, and once when he drove me out west to see the Grand Canyon and the Painted Desert. In those days before motels what I enjoyed most was spending the night with him in cabins along the way.

After the mosquitoes were brought under control at last, his feelings were completely reversed. When my mother died in 1938 she left the town house, built from her monumental earnings, to him and "The Rafters" to her estate to be sold. However, with the enthusiastic support of his children, he made a trade with the estate and kept "The Rafters."

One of the early events I recall was the arrival for the summer of my violin teacher, Mr. Heifetz, the father of Jascha. It is difficult to picture a more incongruous presence in this bucolic backwater than his. His dress was rigidly formal, his trousers often striped, his collar invariably stiff. For reasons not entirely clear, I was required to take walks with him along the rutted dirt roads, a ritual that never failed to evoke catcalls and jeers from the local bumpkins. During my daily lessons he drank hot tea from a glass, Russian-style, filtered through a lump of sugar which he popped into his mouth in advance. He held his bow in readiness at all times, cracking it down on my knuckles periodically for what he called "making mischiefs." At ten years old I must have possessed a genuine talent, if not for the violin, at least for provoking him, for after less than a month he flew into a purple rage, knocked over the music stand and strode up the stairs. Bow in hand, he marched along the balcony to the door of his room where he stopped to deliver a jeremiad in vigorous, albeit non-Oxfordian English. That evening "The Rafters" had a vacancy.

The hill on which our house is situated dished up, for seemingly inexplicable reasons, a rich broth of artists, writers and scholars. This was not in the remotest sense a "colony," and yet an undue proportion of literati chose it as the ideal place to put down roots and go to work. My parents bought our house from Charles Rand

Kennedy, a playwright and Greek scholar who built an outdoor Greek theatre in the woods where his wife, Edith Wynn Matheson, gave performances.

Another playwright and screenwriter, Edward Childs Carpenter and his wife, Helen, lived below us at the end of a meadow. Carp, one of the dearest men I ever knew, had a long career, *The Major and the Minor* being one of his best-known films. It was adapted from a play of his, *Connie Goes Home,* and marked the American directorial debut of Billy Wilder. Before we bought ours, "the Carps", as everyone called them, purchased their lovely old house completely furnished with New England antiques along with four hundred acres, for ten thousand dollars!

The third representative of the lively arts was Laura Hope Crews, a highly successful Hollywood character actress. I never met her, but the public was well acquainted with her out-of-breath portrayals and would long remember Aunt Pittypat in *Gone With The Wind.*

The leftward outlook was represented by the Barnes family whose patriarch, Professor Earl Barnes, used to plow behind a horse when I was a boy. One of their sons, Joseph, who spoke perfect Russian without a trace of accent, went on to become foreign editor of the *New York Herald Tribune* and eventually editor of *Simon & Schuster.* The oldest, Howard, was movie and later drama critic for the *Tribune* while Bernard, the youngest, held the top advertising post at *Time.*

Distinguished novelist and lawyer Walter Gilkyson, chosen late in life to be a clerk at the Nuremberg trials, lived in one of the prettiest of all the old houses with his wife, Bernice Kenyon, the poet and librettist.

An unforgettable couple were Horace and Gertrude Middleton. English both, she trod the unremarkable path of housewife up to the age of sixty when, like Grandma Moses, she suddenly displayed a brilliant gift for portraiture in bronze, turning out an exceptional body of work up to the day she died. Middie, as her husband was called, was short in stature, with a mane of white hair framing a noble brow bereft, as was his entire face, of wrinkles. His eyes were olive-shaped, betraying his linkage to Cornwall where the Phoenicians had come to mine the tin, and had left their genetic imprint upon the land.

Middie had three careers in his life: musicologist and teacher at the Bennett School; co-inventor of a radio process called super-heterodyne; and for the last thirty years, compiler of a dictionary defining all the terms used throughout the entire canon of James Joyce. For the latter task he was formidably endowed, what with his musical expertise, mastery of the classical languages and near-fluency in French, Italian and German.

With all the demands of his agenda he was never too busy to lay down his pen, light his pipe and greet the young lad who had just hopped off his bicycle. He delighted in explaining to me the infinite variety of devices Joyce availed himself of, such as stream of consciousness, multilayered and contrapuntal constructions, puns, double entendres and suggestion of meaning by association. The fact that there was not the slightest chance of his finishing the work in his lifetime was of no consequence at all.

Then, there was the father of my close friend and constant tennis rival, Dick Ludlam. Dick and his brother Paul pursued business careers but their father was the noted Shakespearean actor, Henry Ludlam, to whom Richard Mansfield bequeathed his sword. The story brought to mind the famous *Ifland* ring, traditionally passed on by the greatest German actor in the evening of his career, to his heir apparent. After a long history it came down, through Moissi, to Bassermann who, not deeming any follower worthy of it, had it tossed into his own grave.

Atop the hill lay the sprawling, comfortable domain of the Ellsworth family, dubbed "Esperanza." William Webster Ellsworth, whom I knew as an old gentleman, was editor of *Century* magazine and as such, host to many distinguished visitors. The original village had been built almost across the road from "Esperanza's" future site but, as was the case with many such hamlets, met its fate by fire. When it came to rebuilding, the former inhabitants followed the lead of numerous industrial towns in New England, relocating three miles to the north on the banks of a river.

It happened that one of the guests at "Esperanza" was Arnold Toynbee, who wandered over to the old site and sat down to contemplate what had become of the robust spirit responsible for turning New England into such a pinnacle of human achievement. Lillian Ludlam, Dick's widow, showed me the article the great historian wrote for our local paper in which he cited exploration as the lifeblood of civilization. Only the strongest, the most imaginative and the bravest, he reminded us, start out in the first place; and only the hardiest and most determined survive to put down new roots. So don't look for the spirit of New England in New England, he cautioned; look, rather, in Ohio, Indiana, Illinois, Kentucky and points west. The ones who survive in New England are the ones who stayed home, ultimately to be reinvigorated themselves by the westward migration of new strains from Europe.

Following the sale of the Fishers Island house, "The Rafters" came to be used more and more throughout the year. Every Christmas season Mother's closest friends, "the group," would arrive for a fortnight of walks, feasting and two tables of bridge. They all live in my memory but, as a duffer, I should pay homage to Jim and Frances Whigham, she the daughter of Charles Blair Macdonald, patriarch of American golf. In 1895 Macdonald had been the most influential member of the newly formed United States Golf Association and, at the age of forty, had won the first Amateur Championship sponsored by the organization. His son-in-law would outdo him as a player, however, twice winning the United States Amateur title.

My memory particularly honors Frank Crowninshield, editor of *Vanity Fair*, of whom it was said when he died that the last gentleman was gone. Crowny was always exceptionally kind and encouraging to Maria and me, taking us out occasionally to lunch or tea and making us feel like the most important people on earth. That was his special gift. There were two thousand who received Frank Crowninshield's personally dedicated Christmas card every year, each one of whom considered him his closest friend.

Not a rich man, Crowny was nevertheless one of the earliest and most important American collectors of French impressionism. Toward the end of his life he sold his paintings for several million dollars, an enormous sum at the time. The next morning, demonstrating the sparkling wit for which he was known, he phoned Frances Whigham to say, "Frances, I've never been able to afford you before. Will you be my mistress"?

My father had a studio on the hill. There he spent his days practicing, composing and preparing his violin recitals for the coming season. He was a tireless world traveler, having been, in his estimation, the first to open up the Orient to western music. From 1920 on he returned every two years, including China, Japan, Java, Singapore and Siam in his regular schedule.

In the early thirties he set out on a precedent-setting thirty-day concert tour of South America by airplane, a hazardous undertaking in those days. It was on that occasion that a solid gold cane enclosed in tortoiseshell was presented to him by the dictator of Venezuela, Juan Vicente Gomez, whose heart was softened by Daddy's playing. The cane reposed in a Tokugawa chest in his studio on the hill along with snuffboxes, inros and other companions of his travels.

My father was a voracious reader and possessed a glittering collection of first editions, including a quarto of Shakespeare and the only manuscript in existence of Shaw. He and my mother had many literary friends but Edna St. Vincent Millay was a particular friend of my father's. She and her husband, Eugene Boissevain, visited "The Rafters" several times and on one occasion Daddy set a group of her poems to music. She knew nothing at all about music but she did know how she wanted the songs to sound, and he was able to match the notes and rhythm to her cadences as she read. The result was a charming suite of children's songs.

Meanwhile, paved roads had come to our hill and the party line had gone its way. No longer would we be summoned to the phone by the familiar _ _ •••, nor would a certain Mrs. Atwood be able to stay abreast of everyone's business. In the course of time Charlie Anderson, cheek ever bulging with cut plug, built us a swimming pool, nailing together a wooden frame into which he poured, unassisted, wheelbarrow-full upon wheelbarrow-full of concrete. Two red clay tennis courts were subsequently added shortly before my mother's tragically early death which would, until the opening years of World War II, leave "The Rafters" rudderless.

Two

IN 1935 MY FATHER, WHO HAD BEEN BORN IN RUSSIA but had left long before the Revolution, was invited to give a series of violin recitals in the Soviet Union. As this was a summer tour which coincided with school vacation, my sister Maria and I were brought along at considerable sacrifice, I'm sure, on our parents' part.

The tour was an unqualified triumph. Never in my life have I seen such acclamation. My father was literally carried through the streets on the shoulders of singing, cheering throngs. Considering that these were, musically, the most highly educated audiences in the world, the impact of seeing my beloved father so honored and revered remains with me to this day undiminished. I am particularly haunted by memories of the Mendelssohn and of a mazurka of Chopin, plangent and intoxicating, offered up as an encore under the stars in Sochi, the jewel of the "Russian Riviera."

My mother, who was suffering from the illness that would claim her life a scant three years later, preceded my father to Baden-Baden for the curative waters, but not before setting in operation a plan that had been in development through the summer months: Maria and I were to be left behind in the Soviet Union for the coming academic year. Furthermore, to forestall our frittering away the time, Maria was entered as a piano student in the Moscow Conservatory while I was similarly installed in Kiev, judged to be a safe distance away.

The final concert of the tour was in Moscow. During those highly charged hours my father took me to the bank, where he deposited to our account his entire earnings from the summer. These were paper rubles to be sure, with no value whatever outside the country but within the Soviet Union, a princely sum. "You might as well spend it before you leave," he advised, "because if you don't it will probably buy a bomb."

In the days prior to the opening of the conservatory I made a short trip to Leningrad. There at the Hotel Astoria I was having lunch one day and chatting with the headwaiter who spoke twelve languages. (Russians are among the best linguists in the world, their own tongue and orthography being so complex as to render those of other lands child's play by comparison.) Having yet to learn Russian, which my sister and I would later become fluent in, I was conversing with the captain in English, prompting a nearby diner to join me after the former had withdrawn. Since my Russian at this point consisted of twenty or thirty Berlitz phrases at best and my companion's English being no better, we engaged each other with a mishmash of sounds and signs impossible to reproduce, the tenor of which was:

"What you do in Soviet Union?"

"I come from America with father and mother."

"What father do?"

"He musician—Zimbalist." As there were still billboards throughout the city testifying to his latest appearance I felt it unnecessary (let alone impossible) to elucidate.

"What orchestra he in?"

"He not in orchestra. Some time play with orchestra."

"People come listen?"

"Yes."

"Enjoy?"

"Seem to."

"Where he do this?"

"Here in Leningrad? Philarmonie Hall." There followed a series of further probings which signaled his total bewilderment, capped by a final, anguished protestation which I was forced to engage the good offices of the headwaiter to translate. What was sticking in his craw was: "How is it possible to stand up; before a Soviet audience; right here in Leningrad; in a noted and respected concert hall; with no orchestra at all; and play the cymbals (Zimbalist)"?

I had a fleeting vision of my father clashing and clanging away to both sides of a packed house, and of the worshipful few tiptoeing into the green room afterwards to view, and perhaps even touch, his cymbals.

Kiev was considered, with the possible exception of Leningrad/St. Petersburg, the most beautiful of Russian cities and, with Novgorod, one of the oldest. Founded by the mercantile Vikings, it was wiped out by the Nazis in their Ukraine campaign but rebuilt after World War II, I'm told, with expert and loving care.

I found the city enchanting; my problem was with my curriculum. I had studied the violin and after eight years attained a modest proficiency. On the other hand I had never had a piano lesson yet here I was, aged sixteen, in a piano class with superbly gifted little children, including one *Wunderkind* of four who sat on three telephone books and played like Horowitz.

To make matters worse all classes were conducted in Ukrainian, the coinage of the realm, which bears little or no resemblance to Russian and of which I understood not one word. I was told at the outset I had to take an elective course, my choice being limited to several social and political science subjects—hardly appetizing to me—and German.

It so happened that in my final year at boarding school I was taking second-year German when I came down with the mumps. Confined to the hospital and unable to attend classes I reasoned that, since I had already learned the vagaries of German syntax, including the cluster of verb forms that swarm around the ends of sentences like folds about the ankles in a pair of dropped trousers, I merely needed to increase my vocabulary. Consequently I set about memorizing the dictionary and so had little trouble with the finals. Here at the conservatory I chose German with a purpose: It was for me a mirror exercise, for while my classmates were learning German I was picking up a little Ukrainian.

For a time I was sustained by the stimulation of life at the conservatory and the unfolding of the beauty and tradition of the city. I tried to find a rationale for the course I was launched upon, but with each passing week the utter hopelessness of ever catching up with my class; my inability to comprehend my teachers; and an unremitting sense of alienation combined at last to bring me to a decision: I called my sister to say I was moving to Moscow.

Rail travel in the Soviet Union offered three types of accommodation: international (or first class); *myakhi* (soft), or second class, with an upholstered seat; and *tvyordi* (hard), third class, in which the passenger sat or lay on a plank. The trip to Moscow was an overnight one, with the only available space in third. The boards, roughly two-and-a-half by five feet, were stacked in series of three the length and breadth of the car, mine being at the top. This was my home for the entire journey and, while I soon grew to enjoy the Chekhovian flavor of my surroundings, I found it somewhat of a challenge to avoid skittering off like a hockey puck every time the engineer made a turn or applied the brakes.

For sustenance we would contrive to extricate ourselves at station stops and funnel out to the platform and the quilted woman at the potbellied stove who dispensed sandwiches and hot tea. Climbing back to one's purchase aloft with these in hand without scalding the comrades below required a nicety of timing, balance and precision worthy of a tightrope artiste.

My sister was living *en pension* with a family of four and had procured for me a room with another family directly across the hall. She continued at her conservatory for some time. She was an accomplished pianist, artist and singer, but eventually the malaise of my life infected hers as well, with a corresponding loss of purpose.

One factor in all this is worth mentioning: We had come to the USSR for a summer vacation in the semi-tropics and had, accordingly, brought only the lightest of clothes. Now we were facing a Moscow winter (which had done in Napoleon and was about to do the same to Hitler) with no warm clothes and none to be bought. A Russian with a ration card had to wait a minimum of five years for a pair of shoes, and we had no ration card.

Visitors to the Soviet Union booked their tour in advance through Intourist, with all expenses prepaid in the country of origin. Any extra purchases were financed in *valyuta,* or a gold-backed currency. For these travelers merchandise was readily available, and they were treated quite differently from ordinary Russians by a gold-hungry autocracy. On the other hand, the only goods obtainable by those on rubles without a ration card were luxuries, mainly from the *ancien régime.* Maria bought a fur coat and some jewelry; I, a hideously ugly fur coat and a piano. Fortunately, we had brought along evening clothes, but the laces to my patent leather shoes soon broke from almost nightly use. Since there was not another pair of laces, let alone shoes, to be had the length and breadth of the Soviet Union, I had to depend on Maria's largesse to remove those from a pair of navy blue shoes of hers and lend them to me for the evening.

Our days began, typically, about two P.M. with the arrival of our Russian teacher and a brunch consisting mainly of tea, toast and a pound of caviar which cost the same as butter. Following this collation came the Russian lesson which, as our aptitude increased, became more and more weighted with Russian literature and art. About five o'clock the teacher, a most accomplished woman, would depart and we would begin preparing for the evening. All curtains in Moscow were at seven sharp so at six we would meet on the landing between our apartments, Maria with the laces in hand. After I had performed the necessary transfer we would be off—in a taxi, if the roads were clear, or a sleigh when the snow was piled high. It might be the theatre, the ballet, the opera or the symphony, but rare was the evening we failed to attend a performance of some kind.

After the final curtain our wont was to head for the Metropol bar, watering place for the diplomatic types and foreign correspondents, among whom an uneasy camaraderie prevailed; uneasy because one never knew, in Stalin's Russia, who might overhear and report an unguarded comment. Generally by two A.M. everyone had run out of things to say or was no longer able to articulate them, and the party would start breaking up. Maria and I would head back to our respective abodes, pausing on the landing while I removed, somewhat unsteadily, the laces from my shoes before planting a good-night kiss on her cheek; though I confess there were times when I missed her face altogether.

Three

THERE WERE THIRTY OR FORTY THEATRES IN Moscow, headed by the famed First Art. The world-acclaimed company, crown jewel of the Soviet theatre, actually had in its repertoire, in addition to the classics, an anticommunist play, *The Night of The Turbins*. This astonishing paradox was due to the fact that the eccentric Stalin had been charmed by the play and subsequently countermanded any and all efforts to have it scratched. The presentations of this magnificent company, reflecting the influence of Chekhov, Tolstoy, Gorky and Stanislavsky, were unsurpassed.

Equally stunning were the opera and ballet productions of the Bolshoi. For the great ballroom scene in *Eugene Onegin* for example, chandeliers, costumes and jewelry were lent by the Hermitage and the Catherine Palace. The effect, combined with Tchaikovsky's score, the majesty of the opera house, the great orchestra and magnificent performing artists, was overwhelming.

So much for the cream. In contrast, wth the exception of the Maly and the first-rate Kamerny, the vast majority of remaining theatres varied from mediocre to abysmal. Theirs were the propaganda plays, their currency a kind of Soviet boosterism, their heroes Stakhanovites and the like. I recall one final tableau, representative of most:

The hero and heroine were standing in front of a tractor as he announced, portentously, "Next year I'm going to exceed my norm by twenty paercent!" To which she replied, "And I'm going to exceed mine by twenty-seven!" BLACKOUT. Enough said.

As our clothing problems multiplied, often forcing us to crouch huddled before the radiator, we began to write home begging for warm things. Meanwhile, Christmas (totally ignored, of course, throughout the country) came and went. William Bullitt, friend of Roosevelt and American ambassador to Moscow, who despised the USSR and communism to the point of disdaining to learn a word of Russian, gave a Christmas ball worthy of the tsars (or commi-"tsars," for that matter). He had the entire ballroom floor of Spasso House, the U.S. embassy, removed. Soft lights were installed, on top of which were placed hundreds of hollow, bathroom tile-sized glass cubes filled with water containing tropical fish, which formed a smooth, vitreous surface for dancing. As an ironic touch, Santa Claus was represented by one of the babushkas employed by the trolley lines to sweep the tracks, complete with besom.

Our appeals for clothing grew in frequency and intensity while winter turned to slush, mud and, at last, reluctant spring. (We were to learn in the end that Mother had tried repeatedly to send us packages but each time they were returned as undeliverable.) Then suddenly one day when our spirits were at their lowest, an envelope arrived which left us breathless: enclosed were two Cunard steamship tickets from Le Havre to New York!

When we managed at last to gain a measure of equanimity we set about determining what needed to be done in preparation for our journey. On entering the Soviet Union one's cash was counted and duly recorded; and that was the amount—not a penny more—that was permitted to be taken out upon departure. My parents had entered the Soviet Union from the Orient via the Trans-Siberian

Railroad. Maria and I, on the other hand, had arrived in Leningrad on a Soviet ship from England, escorted by Ruth Dodge, a friend of Mother's. For whatever reason, Maria had brought no money in with her, while I had a five-dollar bill in my wallet which was still in my possession. In addition I had a check on a London bank for the equivalent of twenty dollars.

We ascertained that the cheapest tickets from Warsaw to Paris would cost seventy-five dollars, and since what remained of our resources in rubles—about half—was worthless beyond the frontier, fund-raising suddenly became the order of the day. It was at this very juncture that our fortunes received a leg-up from an unexpected source.

The ruble had been floating comfortably on the black market at around forty to the dollar when out of the blue, word filtered down of the government's intention to peg it arbitrarily at seven. The news threw the foreign contingent into near-panic: They found themselves suddenly in desperate need of rubles. Maria and I had struck up a friendship with the Austrian correspondent who agreed, one night at the Metropol, to trade seventy-five dollars, the most he felt he could risk, for three thousand rubles. This was a dangerous undertaking since he couldn't trust us any more than we could him. Each side could only hope it wasn't walking into a trap.

He gave us his address, the plan being that precisely at midnight I was to step through the front door of his building, which would be ajar, and the exchange would be made inside. As I started off in a taxi my feelings were mixed: Half of me was scared to death while the other half thrilled at the thought that I was not watching a Hitchcock movie—I was starring in it!

I stopped the cab two blocks away and told the driver to wait. I passed no one on the street approaching the building, which was on a corner and totally dark save for the faint glow of a street lamp.

Opening the door wide enough to enter, I was able to make out a curtain ahead of me stretching from one side to the other. This was not uncommon to see in overpopulated Moscow where an entire family was often limited to half a room, with a mere scrim separating them from their neighbors. What happened next was almost instantaneous: As I approached the curtain a hand shot out through a slit; in it was a fifty dollar bill, a twenty and a five. These I seized, replacing them with the rubles and I was gone. Not a word had been spoken.

Back in Maria's room we went to work. With the blinds drawn she emptied out half the contents of a cold cream jar while I wrapped the fifty dollar bill in wax paper. This she placed in the jar, putting back the cold cream to conceal it. Next, we removed the rear plate of an alarm clock, inserted the twenty and put the clock back together. That left the five which I placed in my wallet, not considering it important enough to worry about.

On our last night in Moscow we went to the Kamerny. The chief cook and bottle washer there was a man named Rubinstein. We knew him fairly well, so when he asked us to deliver a letter to Katherine Cornell we readily agreed.

The next morning our spirits were soaring as we boarded the train, bound for home and freedom. A giddy feeling of ecstasy swept us along all the way to the Polish border and our last encounter with a Soviet bureaucrat. This inspector of custom quickly dismissed Maria and directed his full attention to me. At his request I opened my wallet and produced the two five dollar bills and the check. After consulting his records and verifying that I had come in with five dollars, he returned one of the bills to me. The other one, however, he picked up saying, "I take this."

Fighting back the impulse to comment on the smallness of his soul I awaited his next move.

"What this?" he asked, examining the check. I explained what it was.

"I take th—," he started to say before I interrupted him, pointing out that that money was in England and had never been within a thousand miles of his country. "I take this," he repeated.

"No, you do not!" I retorted, seizing the check and tearing it up: a Pyrrhic victory perhaps, but rather satisfying after a year of being on the other end of it.

Back on the train it was time to take stock of our situation; we had a two-day journey ahead of us and the exchequer was totally depleted. This meant no food until we reached Paris, nor were there berths to be made up for the night. On the other hand our seats were reasonably comfortable, our tickets securely in hand and our compartment small enough, with only four seats, to afford a degree of privacy.

The first morning without breakfast was a bit hard but we made it through the day reminding ourselves that we were halfway there. It was the following morning that was more difficult, even though we were close to the end of our journey. We had been traveling alone for some time and were now stopped at a town near the Franco-Belgian border. Starting up again we were joined by a peasant couple, elderly and stiff of joint from years of bending to the soil. He had brought with him an old paper bag from which, after a spell, he extracted with gnarled fingers a fat loaf of heavily crusted bread which he broke, offering her a thick chunk. Next, he brought forth a slab of ham and reaching into his pocket for a penknife proceeded to hack off pieces which they shared, with alternating mouthfuls of bread. What made this almost intolerable for us was not only that they never offered us any, but that their arthritic ways cast the whole maddening performance in slow motion, doubling or tripling our term of suffering.

Time, however, was on our side; for before he had finished the last mouthful and was still wiping his greasy fingers on the bag we were pulling into the station in Paris. To our great relief we were met by an agent from Cook's who had been engaged by Mother to take care of all business, see to our luggage and escort us to our hotel where we found a generous check to provide for our needs before sailing.

That night after a bath and a fabulous dinner we went to see *Top Hat*. If ever there was an antidote to the gray face of communism it was that film; and I am eternally grateful to have been given the privilege, years later, of thanking both Fred Astaire and Ginger Rogers for leading two bone-weary, bedraggled young wayfarers into the sparkling sunlight with their magic.

On board the *Aquitania* Maria and I had finished dinner and were taking a stroll on deck. As we paused to look over the rail I drew Rubinstein's letter from my pocket. We exchanged a look—it was enough. Taking it from me and opening it carefully she began to read:

"My dear Miss Cornell: I send you greetings from the Soviet Union by the hand of two dreadful children who have behaved disgracefully in our great fatherland . . ."

I did go to see Katherine Cornell in New York. She was appearing in Shaw's *St. Joan* with a cast that included an unknown young man named Tyrone Power. Dropping backstage afterwards I delivered Rubinstein's greetings to her.

But on the deck of the *Aquitania* I took the letter and, with perhaps a touch of the ham, tore it into little pieces which we watched, lingeringly, as the wind lifted and wafted them far, far out into the night.

Our thoughts were not on the letter. They were thousands of miles to the east, raising a glass to a kindly and generous people, warm and trusting, brilliantly creative and tortured of soul, who had never in their history tasted freedom; and to an interpretation of life we would never share again.

Four

THERE WAS A PERIOD IN MY LIFE BETWEEN 1934 AND 1938 that included the Soviet experience, a period which, much as I would dearly love to ignore it, will not allow me to. It is a time of which I am not proud and which I would give almost anything to undo or relive, were such an option offered to us non-reincarnationists. I bring it up now because I find that, were I not to, the picture of me which might otherwise emerge would be disingenuous.

It is customary in this day of bearded opinions to cite an array of external reasons for lapses in one's customary behavior. While this may be valid in some cases, it is utterly inadequate as a means of explaining mine. I can only suggest that a person may conceivably let go of the reins for no more profound reason than to scratch.

At St. Paul's School, although the discipline was severe, far from suffering under it I enjoyed the school immensely. The fact that girls were only allowed on the campus one weekend a year; that the few biddies employed by the school were toadlike and long-of-tooth; that everything imaginable was prohibited, with the tiniest infraction of the rules resulting in instant dismissal; that our allowance was limited to from one to three dollars a month; and that during that period the town of Concord, New Hampshire was accessible but once, and then only aboard the supervised school bus—none of this did I find unbearable or crushing to my spirit.

That six of us decided to form a clandestine smoking ring was due not to the school's "oppressive" regimen but rather, as far as I can analyze it, to nothing more than a childish thirst for adventure. We would meet after dark in one of the cabalists' rooms (usually mine) with a fire escape outside the window, where we would make the most peculiar preparations for the night. These consisted of rubbing mud over our clothes, faces and hands in a naïve attempt at camouflage and which, had we been spotted by accident, would only have served to make us stand out as curiously dirty SPS boys.

Having hopped off the fire escape, we would proceed stealthily to a clearing in the woods where we had, during daylight hours, buried a large jar filled with cigarettes and matches. Here in the crackling New Hampshire night we would squat, huddled in a tight circle for warmth, light up and act for all the world as though nirvana had enfolded us in its silken embrace. The thrill, of course, had nothing to do with smoking, but rather with the knowledge that we were getting away with something which, were it known to our innocent classmates, would leave them bug-eyed with envy and admiration.

On two occasions we actually made it into Concord where, in addition to smoking, we drank beer and (I blush to recall it!) danced with girls to the throbbing accompaniment of a juke-box.

One night on our way to a smoking tryst toward the end of the school year, four had already descended from my fire escape, leaving Jimmy Hundley and me to follow when to our horror, we heard my house master, one Craig Wylie, knocking his way down the hall checking beds. Jimmy dived underneath mine while I scrambled to pull the covers over me just as Wylie opened the door. He must have spotted one too many hands or feet for after a long pause he remarked, sarcastically, "Well, excuse ME, boys," and left.

The implication was outrageous, as he well knew. Being caught smoking was the most grievous offense one could possibly commit but this was worse. After cleaning up I knocked on his door and said, "Sir, what we were doing was not what you thought. We were on our way to smoke cigarettes."

"What you were on your way to do," he all but sneered, "is not of the slightest interest to me. If you have something to confess you'll have to do it to the Rector." The next day an ad hoc committee of six met hurriedly and decided that this was, in fact, our only alternative. In drawing lots the unhappy choice fell upon me.

Dr. Samuel S. Drury was an ordained minister whose stamp, as headmaster, made itself felt in every facet of school life, from the chapel—the center of our existence—to the classroom and even to the playing field. He was an imposing, if not terrifying, figure, with eyes that seemed to penetrate through you and well into the plaster beyond.

The sun danced through the blinds of his study window as he sat behind the desk, gently rocking. "I understand you have something you want to tell me," he said.

"Yes, sir."

"Well, what is it?"

"Last night, sir, six of us met in my room. Four had gone down the fire escape when Mr. Wylie opened the door, discovering the two of us who were left. He implied that something improper was taking place."

"And was it?"

"No, sir."

"What was taking place?"

"Well the fact is, sir, we had planned to smoke cigarettes."

"I see. Suppose you tell me about it."

Conscious of his eyes boring through me, I recounted to the best

of my ability the events leading up to the house master's entrance
into my room.

"Is this the only occasion you've done anything like this?" he
asked.

"No, sir." I described the routine of the fire escape, the camouflage
and the jar buried in the woods.

"How many times have you done this?"

Feeling that trying to deceive him would be as futile as trying to
outwit an X-ray machine I answered, "About twenty-five."

After a pause he asked, "Is that all you've done?"

"No, sir."

"What else?" I described the expeditions into Concord, not omit-
ting the girls and the beer. At last, from him: "Do you have anything
more to tell me?"

"No, sir."

Three minutes must have elapsed while I sat, wringing wet from
the ordeal. Finally he remarked, his features softening almost imperceptibly,

"You feel better now, don't you?"

"No, sir," I said, "I feel terrible."

The incredible happened: Not one further word was ever mentioned of the affair and we all went on to graduate. In the years before his death I used to visit Dr. Drury on Martha's Vineyard where
he and his wife spent their summers, and after he was gone, dropped
in on her from time to time. He was one of the giants. I've known a
few in my day, but none stood taller than he.

It would seem a foregone conclusion that the lessons I learned from
the above-mentioned episode, yoked with the generosity shown me
and the hairbreadth escape I experienced, would serve to hold me to

a bearing of probity for many years to come. Such, however, was not the case. Following a time of unsupervised license in the USSR, I entered Yale more in the footsteps of Till Eulenspiegel than with any seriousness of purpose, thirst for knowledge or desire to vindicate my parents' faith in me. Moreover, the devastating effect of the stock market crash on their fortunes (the extent of which, in point of fact, I knew nothing about until years later when my older sister Marcia told me of it) was something I never even considered. By this time my mother who had earned many millions of dollars was in retirement, and my father, whose career, to be sure, was at its zenith, had nonetheless the entire financial weight of the family resting squarely on the fingers of his left hand and his bowing arm. There were no more investments to help out.

Within days of my arrival at Yale I met Chandler Cowles, who had been kicked out the previous year and was now what was known as a "social sophomore"—in reality a repeating freshman. Chandler, who would become my closest friend for life, had in his nature that-which instantly struck a chordal note with my insatiable craving for adventure. We brought out in terms of academic orthodoxy the worst in each other and yet, despite the regrettable outcome of our association at Yale, would survive to bring out the very best.

Outside the gates of Yale, Harvard and Princeton lay the finest tailoring in the United States and I in particular fell victim to the siren song of its vendors, opening charge accounts (and making full use of them) in all their stores. "Come on over, Ef," they would say, dropping in on me at Vanderbilt Hall where I lived. "Think of us as your private club, whether you buy anything or not. And remember, you don't have to pay for a whole year." Sportcoats of Irish, English and Scottish tweed were my greatest weakness, although the haberdashery and shoe departments hardly failed to escape my attention.

Chandler and I, surely the most naïve and innocent members of our class, lived in a fantasy world, the world of "supposing that." Our days consisted of dreaming up exploits of sophisticated derring-do, pretending we were international spies, *soigné* gigolos or movie heroes.

Chandler's Aunt Mary, the widow of a manufacturer of automobile door handles, lived a comfortable life of quiet reminiscence in a shaded, faintly lavender-scented house off Chapel Street. She possessed an ancient Cadillac limousine which Chandler, at his most charming, attempted fruitlessly to persuade her to part with. He was more successful in his efforts to con the sweet old lady, who adored him, out of the occasional tenner when needed, prompting her to exclaim in the spirit of the game, "Dear me suds, Chan Cowles, you're a caution!"

Our most daring exploit (and the one with the most far-reaching consequences) grew, like the others, out of our immaturity and complete lack of worldliness. Attending a movie which included a burlesque show we each selected, as if we were Ziegfeld, the pair of legs in the chorus most to our liking, and gave ourselves the assignment of meeting the rest of the girl to whom they belonged. His girl's name was Virginia Dixon, a brunette, and mine, Virginia Swanson, a blonde with a slight gap between her front teeth. Rebuffed at the stage door we reasoned that the company must be staying at one of the hotels in town.

Thumbing through the telephone book we called every single one, hitting pay dirt with the very last, the Hotel Garde, across the railroad tracks. Checking into a room we ordered a bottle of Scotch to give us nerve. I gulped down half of it before handing it to Chandler and immediately began to feel sick. When he managed to reach the girls on the phone I was dimly aware of his giving them our names and room number as the ceiling started to swirl around me.

Lying back on the carpetlike bedspread I was only able, as they came in the door, to raise my head before passing out cold.

We were utterly inexperienced in the unfeeling, calculated ways employed by the man-about-town in dealing with pickups such as these. Accordingly we treated them like duchesses, affording them a huge, and certainly much needed, boost to their self-esteem. We lavished flowers and presents on them, including a beautiful alligator bag from Dunhill's I remember giving V.S. Our puppylike artlessness seemed to both girls to be a happy relief from the somewhat squalid routine of their life, as Chandler and I wined and dined them throughout their New Haven run and on to Philadelphia and beyond.

As might have been anticipated the effect upon our classwork at Yale, already sorely neglected and substandard was, quite simply, terminal. Upon our return Chandler was kicked out for the second time and I for the first. Before I left, my brother-in-law Russell Davenport, one of the pillars of Henry Luce's publishing empire and my all-but-brother, arrived in New Haven. A distinguished graduate of Yale, he was able to persuade the authorities to give me another chance the following year.

Sadly, I learned no more from my failings as a freshman than I had from escaping disaster at St. Paul's: My appetite for testing the limits seemed insatiable. Throughout my first year, having rapidly overrun my limit of cuts, I had stormed the dispensary with an encyclopedia of pretended ailments, affording me a better preparation for an acting career than anything I subsequently undertook. Once in the middle of winter after taking a hot shower I stood out on my balcony at Vanderbilt in shorts in order to catch cold.

In my crowning performance I complained of an occasional stabbing pain in my lower right side. Unable in those days to prove or disprove the existence of appendicitis merely from those symptoms, the doctor suggested I enter the hospital for a few days to await developments. "Or," he added, "you could rest at home."

"Perhaps that would be best," I answered pluckily. Chandler and I took off for "The Rafters" and a rollicking three days.

The first time I visited the dispensary as a "social sophomore," the doctor pulled out my medical record. After scanning it he said, "Mr. Zimbalist, last year you showed up here forty-three times with various symptoms, from headaches, abdominal pains, spinal dislocations, muscular aches, to clouded vision and just about everything in between. I'm going to give you a medical excuse this time but this is the last time. I don't want to see your face here ever again."

With my favorite refuge denied me, the effects of my unexcused absences from class began to mount up. I found my professor of European history, which happened to be a subject I enjoyed, inexpressibly boring. He would read in a monotone at breakneck speed from a paper on the lectern before him, for a solid hour never looking up as if to defy us to match his speed with our note-taking.

Equally galling to me was my geology professor. He was a pleasant man and I found nothing wrong with his classes. It was the field trips that chafed, for he would lead us in single file through the streets of New Haven in search of scarps—a tall man in boy scout shorts with a clipboard and a walk like Jacques Tati, up on the toes with each step. We were, as might be imagined, the subject of lively ridicule.

My parents furnished me with a very generous allowance of fifty dollars a month, but with my Tiffany tastes that lasted but a few days. My meals were well provided by the freshman Commons but as it failed to offer the variety my palate deemed necessary, I opened charge accounts at various tea shops and restaurants around town.

Since I couldn't afford laundry I simply charged new shirts, throwing the soiled ones under my bed. At one point I had a collection of more than fifty.

When I was tossed out of Yale the second time I left owing most restaurants and clothing stores in town large amounts of money. In all, many thousands of dollars were involved which, in the currency of today as I write, would be valued at ten to twenty times that figure.

Arriving in New York I was too scared of facing my mother to go home, and found refuge with a kind friend of Chandler's, Bob Steiner, who fed me and let me stay in his small apartment for three months while I looked for work. After being hired at last by NBC as a page, I rented a room for four dollars a week. That's where I was living when, less than a year later, my mother died. I only saw her again when I visited the hospital.

Mother was the most forceful woman I have ever known, and yet she was possessed of such beauty and charm as to be able to exert great influence upon the world around her without arousing the least resentment. The hardness and stridency which often ingrain the personas of strong-minded people were conspicuously absent in her. It was her ways and the weight of her enormous achievements that were winning, not her invective; and her success was in no small part due to being large-minded, never petty. For example, over a game of bridge, she suggested to the chairman of the Hartford utilities company that bringing electricity to our neighborhood would be of benefit to his stockholders as well as to the local population. The next summer, power lines traversed the twenty miles from Hartford to our hill and the lives of thousands were changed.

In the years following her retirement, Mother worked tirelessly on behalf of many causes. She was instrumental in creating the American Guild of Musical Artists (AGMA); and in addition to her charitable works she founded the Musical Art Quartet, whose chamber recitals she underwrote to the end of her life. Much of her energy was spent in support of my father's career (boxes for a Carnegie Hall concert are not sold by serendipity). She entertained lavishly, introducing her guests to the innovative horseshoe-shaped dining-room table which doubled seating capacity and obviated the need for a buffet. Following dinner everybody retired to the enormous redwood-paneled music room of the New York house. There the glitterati of the musical, artistic, literary and social worlds entertained and were entertained by impromptu chamber music, readings and solo performances. My mother's was, in the words of Cleveland Amory, the last salon.

One day Lynn Fontanne, the distaff side of the magnificent Lunts, rang Mother up in a high state of agitation about Rachmaninoff, himself a frequent participant in these soirees. While no Adonis, he exerted a magnetic attraction upon women and Lynn had followed him up and down, in and out of stores on Fifth Avenue like a faithful puppy.

"Alma," she rhapsodized, "you've simply got to give a dinner so I can meet him." Mother obliged, but when introduced to the great pianist and composer, Lynn, who was notoriously myopic, cried,

"No! No! Why, that's not the man at all!" She had been following a complete stranger!

Perhaps the most graphic example of the iron in my mother's character was displayed by her reaction to the stock market crash, which left her with a frightening figure at the bottom of the ledger. Instead of pulling my sister and me out of boarding school, holing up and pinching pennies, in 1930 she took us around the world, first class all the way. We were accompanied by her maid and Sheldon Luce, Henry's undergraduate brother, who was my tutor for the trip. If she was going under, it would be with a statement, not a whimper.

Among my most cherished memories of that wondrous journey, the seven-day crossing to Southampton on the *Majestic* retains a special significance for me. I developed whooping cough the very first day out and was confined to bed most of the time at sea. Reading aloud is an occupation much scorned today, but in my mother it approached the level of an art. Before we landed she had painted my mind with *David Copperfield* and *The Old Curiosity Shop* to the point where, walking off the boat train, I stepped right into Dickens's London. Prepared by a week of insulation at sea and fired by the tracery of my mother's reading, my imagination merged gently into the reality of an old world resistant as yet to the homogenizing influence of the dollar. Surely it is no coincidence that I found myself, many years later, reading a great number of books on tape, including the entire Bible.

I have before me as I write the only diary I ever kept. It chronicles, in a twelve-year-old's words and script, the wonder of that odyssey: Paris and the mirror in which Marie Antoinette beheld herself head-less before the blade of the guillotine descended; all the tourist attractions including Belleau Wood and the World War trenches; the train trip through the Alps to Rome, past Pisa and its tower; getting lost in the Catacombs; countless Cook's tours and sightseeing; bicycling with Sheldon to Ostia and a lunch which included soup with a squid floating around in it; Luna Park, a point of special interest; Florence and Fiesole; and finally Genoa, where my father joined us, having been prevented by his schedule from making the first part of the journey with us.

Down the Mediterranean we sailed on the Dutch ship *Jan Peterzoon Coen*, bound for the East Indies. In Port Said, Egypt, we made a fueling stop during which, as the collier-barge pulled alongside, the workers were flogged with a whip by the foreman, arousing fury among the onlooking passengers. Slipping through the canal at night, we arrived in Suez early in the morning, before crossing the Red Sea and the Gulf of Aden into the Indian Ocean, our decks awash with flying fishes.

Landing in Colombo, the capital of Ceylon, my diary notes that I had two pairs of pants made in two hours. After a day in Sabang, Sumatra, we set sail for Java which we reached in three days, and where I had "the nuts of a time."

I recall that in the Hotel des Indes in Batavia the source of water in the room which Sheldon and I shared consisted of a bucket. In those days before air conditioning, the humid, equatorial heat was fierce. In my exploration of the hotel I discovered an enormous tank filled with cool water into which I hopped, and was luxuriating in the relief it offered. Suddenly my reverie was brusquely interrupted by an angry official who chased me out, crying in a mixture of Malay, Dutch and English that the bucket was to be dipped in the tank, not the boy!

Night was a welcome respite from the heat as we lay in our beds under netting watching the patient lizards on the ceiling trapping mosquitoes with their lively tongues. We explored the island thoroughly in the week we were there, which included a night spent at Surabaya in the mountains where we slept under two blankets!

The *Tjisondari* which conveyed us from Batavia up the China coast was a freighter with a few excellent accommodations for passengers. Only upon arrival did we learn that our cargo had been a human one—tragic, wretched coolies. After a few days in Hong Kong we boarded the Japanese motorship *Tatsuta Maru* bound for Shanghai, Yokohama, and following a week in Japan, on to San Francisco via Honolulu.

We were received in Tokyo by Prince Tokugawa, Japan's last shogun and longtime friend of my father's, and in Honolulu by David, a revered Hawaiian ascetic who lived near the top of Diamond Head and who graciously prepared poi for Maria and me on the dirt floor of his cave.

The world we saw and heard and smelled is gone without leaving a trace, immolated on the slag and cinders of World War II. My debt to the diarist is reserved, however, since in Hong Kong, like a faithless penitent in the closing weeks of Lent, he had laid his pencil aside for other pursuits—and so shall I. It has been a sketchy outline at best of the wondrous gift my mother bestowed upon her children from the warehouse of her crippled resources and failing health. The last nine years of her life she suffered agonizingly from cirrhosis, though she never drank. Nobody but her family and closest friends was aware of it. She refused to allow the disease to dictate her way of life or to spread gloom upon others, while she fought to sustain her customary activities as long as she was able.

As the end approached and she lay helplessly in her hospital bed, she saw the need to make a list of those special objects she wished for each of her three children to receive upon her death. Knowing that the process would destroy my father and that neither Maria nor I was mature enough to go through such an ordeal, she summoned our older sister, Marcia Davenport, to her bedside. Marcia, twice married, had fought her way to the top of the literary world. She certainly possessed the toughness and experience to carry out the assignment, but as the visceral process dragged on and familiar family possessions paraded up and down the page, even she broke down. "Mother," she all but sobbed, "I can't take any more. Do we have to go on with this right now?"

The response was short, blunt—and eloquent: "Who the hell is doing the dying around here?"

Five

 I SUPPOSE THERE ARE THOSE WHO, ON LOOKING back over their lives, can truthfully state that they managed to achieve all their goals without help. I am not one of them. When I entered the army in 1941 I could boast of but one professional engagement, a small part in a half-hour radio show, not a running part, a one-time part; that and a stint in a mumble chorus.

By 1939 I had been a member for two years of the page and guide staff of NBC in Radio City, a confraternity that included such unlikely names as Gordon MacRae, Gregory Peck, the baritone Earl Wrightson and Thomas Merton, the future Trappist. We underwent inspection every morning like marines—uniform, shave, haircut, finger nails; we were the bravest of the brave! As pages, we facilitated the flow of audiences into the radio studios on our floor (there would be, of course, no television until after the war). During program time, a page would stand inside with an ammonia capsule in his pocket, ready to revive anyone who might suddenly find himself horizontal.

We all had our various goals, mine being acting. Consequently, I auditioned ceaselessly, bearding the lair of Donna Butler, the charming and kind-hearted talent coordinator. I read for every single part that came along, finally landing, by dint of perseverance alone, the above-mentioned role on *Renfrew of the Mounted.* It was an epochal moment in my life. I had become in the wink of an eye a professional! Sad to say, my excitement gave way to crushing disappointment when I was informed, a few days later, that NBC had a policy which prohibited employees from appearing on the air. Faced with this cruel dilemma, I wasted little time turning in my uniform and gold braid. The forty dollars I received from *Renfrew of the Mounted* made it all worthwhile!

The occasion of the mumble chorus came about through the kindness of a dear friend of mine, John Stephen, who as skipper of mumble brought both Chandler and me aboard. The program was *Cavalcade of America,* sponsored by DuPont ("Better Things for Better Living Through Chemistry!"). This was far and away the ritziest radio show in town, featuring the Churchillian Homer Fickett as director and a cast of Orson Welles graduates which numbered John McIntire, Jeanette Nolan, Agnes Moorhead, Carl Swenson, Elliott Reid and others including, from time to time, Welles himself. These hourlong dramas were presented onstage in an audience-filled Broadway theatre with the performers clad in tuxedos and long evening gowns—the ultimate in posh. Needless to say, the orchestra in the pit was similarly arrayed.

Meanwhile, off to one side sat the mumble chorus, some twelve of us aspiring thespians in cocktail dresses and dark suits. At an appropriate moment in the action John, with an upward motion of his hands, would bring us to our feet, where we would proceed to spout such remarks as, "Hoist the mizzentop!" or, "Bring'er hard to starboard!" By a circular motion of his arms, he would indicate that our output should continue undiminished, even increasing in intensity as his efforts became more strenuous. At last, by a floppy forward motion of both palms he would indicate a diminuendo, accented ultimately by placing a cautionary forefinger upon his lips. A wiping motion of one hand in front of the neck would inform us that our moment in the sun had come to an end, and we would return to our seats to await the next summons. For these efforts we earned the sum of fifteen dollars a week, on which we all lived quite comfortably, thank-you very much.

While I was still at NBC I would take the train after work to Boonton, New Jersey, to express my artistry in a wretched little stock company in nearby Mountain Lakes, a bus ride away. For our efforts the director, a kind of tontine swindler, contrived to pay us nothing, claiming his expenses were always greater than the box office receipts.

One night, the cast having been held overlong after the curtain by this poor-talking shell game artist, it was too late when we were finally released for me to catch the last train from Boonton. There was, however, one more departure, the final one to New York that night out of Brick Church, scheduled at 12:30. Since bus service had been discontinued by that hour, a couple of actors living near there volunteered to drive me.

It so happened that none of us had a watch. We knew it would be a close call and all I could do was hope and pray we'd get there in time. When they dropped me off I had misgivings, for everything was dark and deserted. This was a typical station, with a building and platform on each side of the tracks separated by a metal fence down the middle. As I paced nervously back and forth, trying to keep my hopes alive, my pulse suddenly quickened at the sight of a car pulling up on the other side. Two men in shirtsleeves emerged and as they stepped onto the opposite platform I yelled, "Do you know what time it is?"

"Yeah," one of them shouted back, "12:25.".

As I heaved a sigh of relief I noticed they were walking out onto the tracks.

"Where are you heading for?" the other one asked and with this, they both began to scale the dividing fence.

"New York," I said, pausing long enough for them to reach my platform.

"What are you doing in Brick Church?"

"I came here from work if it's any of your business." At this my eagerly awaited train began approaching the station.

As it steamed to a stop, the one who appeared to lead the questioning commented, "Isn't it a little late to be coming from work?"

"Aren't you asking a few too many questions?" I replied, turning to board the train.

"You're not getting on there," he said, producing a badge. You're coming with us."

At the police station I was told I'd have to wait for the captain to show up. Any station—railroad, police or military—is a dreary and incommodious place to kill time, and here the ticking pendulum of the Regulator on the wall was my only companion as it tolled the hours, two of them, in jerky, fifteen-second increments. When the poor captain finally arrived after 3:00, rudely levered no doubt from his slumbering lady's side, he settled into an elevated version of a judge's banc where, after glancing at the pertinent papers, he crooked his finger at me. "Young man," he said as I approached, "do you have a driver's license?"

"Yes, sir," I answered, fishing it from my wallet.

Whether he was a music lover or a record collector or had chanced to read a press release I'll never know, but he recognized my father's name instantly. Turning to the arresting officer, he exploded, "You idiot! You stupid idiot! What's the first thing I've told you to ask for? Identification! IDENTIFICATION!!! You've brought a perfectly innocent man in here in the middle of the night for no reason at all! Well, now you're going to have the pleasure of driving him to New

York, yourself!" Turning to me he said, "I'm terribly sorry, Mr. Zimbalist. I apologize for the mistake. I hope you understand."

"As a matter of fact, sir," I replied, "I don't."

"You see," he proceeded to explain, "there was a murder committed in Brick Church this evening. We set up roadblocks and covered all train stations and airports. The fact is you bear quite a resemblance to the description we've received of the murderer."

I thanked him for his performance of duty as I slid into the car alongside the arresting officer who, seething with anger and humiliation, never opened his mouth all the way to New York.

My only other theatrical exposure was at the hands of a woman, the daughter of a successful businessman, who aspired to produce plays which would replace the second feature in movie houses. This lady, determined to prove she didn't need her father's help, was poor as a church-mouse, surviving exclusively on Wrigley's spearmint gum, one stick of which she made do for the whole day.

We rehearsed *Alice in Wonderland,* her first undertaking, in an abandoned mews without heat, in the middle of a New York winter. She had, of course, nothing to pay us with beyond the hope that her idea might find acceptance by some movie theatre chain. I remember very little about my role other than that I was a gardener who turned into a carpet to be trod upon.

She had arrranged for a tryout in a large theatre in New Jersey, which had agreed to suspend its second feature one time in order to test her idea. Our makeshift set was in readiness behind the movie screen as the first feature concluded, followed by an unanticipated development: As no one had thought to publicize our arrival, our poor sponsor not having saved enough Wrigley's to pay for advertising, the whole audience, with the exception of a half-dozen who remained to enjoy their six-packs and hot dogs, got up and walked out.

We had not been underway more than a minute before these aroused Jerseyites, who had had a few beforehand, began hurling insults at us: "Get that crap outa here!" "Go on back where you came from!" "Beat it!"

When our leader decided to proceed regardless, we soon found out what a duck in a shooting gallery must feel like, as we were engulfed in a barrage of hot dogs, french fries, catsup, tomatoes and beer.

Such had been the sum total of my acting career when I was asked, by the army, for my civilian occupation. I suppose I could have cited the publishing business for I had, in fact, worked for *Time* one summer as a mail clerk. One day shortly after I joined the company the phone rang, and being the only one in the room at the time I answered it.

"Who's this?" thundered a voice, which turned out to belong to Roy Larson, the publisher.

"Efrem Zimbalist, sir," I responded.

"Yeah?" he barked. "Well this is Arturo Toscanini. Get your ass up here and sharpen some pencils!"

Upon reflection, I decided it would probably be more judicious to claim acting for my civilian occupation. I spent five years in the army with no chance to gild my résumé. For five years I was forced to answer questions about my theatrical past with: "Oh, a little radio, a little summer stock. You know how it is."

$\mathcal{S}ix$

Emily and I met at the Neighborhood Play-house School of the Theatre. My father and I, following the death of my mother, had taken an apartment together in New York and the first day I laid eyes on Emily I told him, upon returning home, "I've met the girl I'm going to marry." He received this news in the bathtub, covering himself modestly with a washcloth as was his custom.

"Now, Sonny," he replied, "when I was a young man in Russia, I met a ballerina named Galia. I thought I was in love and that I couldn't live without her. But I've lived very nicely without her and married your mother, so you see it's better not to get carried away. You'll have plenty of time to think about this."

Two days later, when she came to dinner at our apartment, he lost his head even more than I had! In fact, the following year while I was in the army and she had reluctantly agreed to my insistence that we defer our plans until the end of the war, he took her out to dinner and said, "Now, Emily, when are you going to marry my son?"

The wedding took place at The Little Church Around the Corner, the actors' church, with Father Ray presiding. Its real name is The Church of the Transfiguration, its sobriquet stemming from another larger church nearby. At the turn of the century actors were not allowed to enter that more fashionable house of worship, and if they showed up they would be met with a polite brushoff and the words, "There's a little church around the corner. You might try there."

Emily was well acquainted with the South when I received orders to report to Infantry Officers' Candidate School at Fort Benning, Georgia. For four months she had toured all the southern camps in the play *Claudia* for the USO.

At Benning we rented a tiny house off the base where I managed to catch infrequent glimpses of her during the ninety days we were there. On graduation I was assigned to Camp McClellan in Anniston, Alabama, whither we headed in the spiffy 1938 Buick Roadmaster convertible sedan I had bought in Connecticut for five hundred dollars. With white sidewall tires, a sleek black body trimmed in red and a brand-new canvas top, it was something to behold!

At McClellan we lived a comparatively normal life after Benning, with one notable exception: Alabama, like many southern states, had package laws, which meant that bars were only permitted to sell setups. The alcoholic component had to be purchased in state-controlled liquor stores and carried to the bar in a paper bag.

During a Saturday night dance at the Officers' Club I was standing at the bar mixing our drinks when, glancing back toward Emily, I saw my commanding officer approaching the table. He, a lieutenant colonel, had been drinking heavily and while I watched in horror, proceeded to maul my wife in an attempt to force himself on her. As I started for him I had little time to consider the consequences: This was wartime and striking a superior officer was a court martial offense of the utmost gravity. Nevertheless there was nothing else I could do.

Emily saw me coming. Being a Navy brat herself she knew what the stakes were. From off the floor she landed a right uppercut on his jaw that catapulted him over the table onto the lap of a nearby lady. Angry and humiliated, he staggered to his feet and out the door. Her quick thinking had saved me.

Even so, I didn't know what to expect the next day at lunch as I passed his table on my way out of the officers' mess. He could have made things very unpleasant for me but he stopped me instead with, "Lieutenant, your wife was quite right to do what she did. I was completely at fault and I want to offer an apology to her and to you."

A couple of weeks later we had a visit from my father. He and Mary Curtis Bok, founder of the Curtis Institute of Music in Philadelphia of which he was director as well as head of the violin department, decided on marriage. Typically, he had flown all the way from Maine for my approval and was about to seek the same from Maria in Reno where she was living. Well aware of his loneliness and knowing Mary as an outstanding, noble and warmhearted lady, Emily and I were thrilled to send him off with our blessing.

After three months at McClellan I was transferred to the Rainbow Division in Muskogee, Oklahoma, for processing before being sent overseas. We were there only two weeks.

When my orders came through I was granted a week's leave before reporting to Camp Kilmer, New Jersey, for embarkation. On arriving there, I would admire the ingenuity of the men who were mailing off letters in the face of the strictest wartime censorship, letters containing messages like, "I think that I shall never see a place as lovely as this again." Or, "The trees here are really lovely. All you can see for miles are trees, trees and more trees."

Meanwhile, the only chance we had of making it to "The Rafters" from Muskogee was to catch a plane from Tulsa. The rub was that the flight in question (there was but one every few days) was scheduled to depart a half-hour before we could reasonably expect to be there.

Jumping into the Buick, we tore up the road at 120 miles per hour for most of the way. I expected every second to be pulled over, but every second turned into a minor miracle. When we reached the airport the plane was pulling out of its berth. Driving onto the field I stopped in its path as we jumped out and started waving furiously. In those days the uniform commanded universal respect, and it did from that pilot, who opened the hatch and let us aboard.

We never saw the car again but a kind friend from McClellan managed to rescue it and sell it. Because of its heroic service we did make it to "The Rafters," which stretched out its arms to us in welcome. During that happy week we both drew heavily on its strength for the days ahead.

Seven

I STEPPED OFF A TROOPSHIP ONTO ENGLISH SOIL A few weeks after D-Day as an infantry replacement officer. Upon arrival I was assigned to a replacement depot—or repple depple, as they were familiarly called—whose function was to fill in the gaps caused by casualties in the front lines. Once the Normandy beachhead had been secured and our troops were able to begin the push inland, my unit began moving southward towards the Channel until the invading forces had cleared the coast by about seventy miles. At that point we were shipped over to France where we maintained this discreet interval, advancing as they advanced. Each day there was roll call and those selected departed to replace the fallen while the rest of us awaited our turn.

As our course progressed unhurried through the French countryside there came a day when we found ourselves fifteen miles from Paris, the closest we would ever be. Thinking this might be my last chance to revisit the city, which had only been liberated a week before, I hit upon a daring plan: All leaves having been canceled, I waited for the daily roll call and when my name didn't appear, took off "over the hill," catching a ride on a charcoal-burning truck bound for Paris. The risk to be sure was great but the

49

potential prize greater, and I felt confident I could be back before roll call the next day. Hopping off at the *Gare St. Lazare,*I checked in at a nearby hotel but had to leave my bag at the desk as the rooms were rented by the hour until 10 P.M.! This was hardly the Ritz but it suited my wallet since the army, quite rightly, gave itself a highly unfavorable rate of exchange so as not to cripple the fragile French economy.

Having paid for my room in advance, I set out in search of a shop where I might find a small painting to send home to my wife Emily. The atmosphere throughout the city was exhilarating beyond belief. The American army was idolized as never before, I daresay, in its history, inundated in a sea of flowers, kisses and embraces. When I returned a year later the mood was markedly different, but for this brief moment it was intoxicating.

I found a store benefiting French prisoners of war and was browsing around, rather intimidated by the prices, when two young ladies offered their assistance. Thanks to them I was able to find a charming little painting which must have cost a great deal more than they charged me. It turned out they were sisters doing charity work for the organization, which had only recently been instrumental in the repatriation of their father, a well-known playwright, from a prison camp. When they invited me to dinner at their home which they shared with their parents I gratefully accepted, little anticipating the problem in logistics I would be facing.

They lived near the Trocadéro, all the way across town and there were no taxis; indeed, with gasoline unavailable, there was little vehicular traffic at all, save for a few charcoal-burning cars and trucks with towerlike structures mounted in the rear—gloriously French in concept—spewing forth noxious fumes. Once again my uniform served as passe-partout when a kindly gentleman stopped obligingly and drove me right to my destination.

The dinner was delightful, the first of many I would share with this distinguished family when I returned to Paris after V E Day for a six-month stay awaiting shipment home. I emerged from their apartment building after midnight to find myself so enshrouded in a pea-soup fog that I was literally unable to see my extended hand in front of me. The streets were totally deserted, as the blinding conditions made driving out of the question. Since there was no alternative I began to walk, feeling my way along the edges of buildings. After a few minutes I realized I was in no danger crossing the street, for the only thing likely to run into me was a dog or cat more confused than I. Groping my way thus foot by foot across a city of no light or sound, I arrived, a little after three, at the corner near my hotel. In an effort to confirm my bearings I bumped into a street lamp, which I was only able to identify by virtue of being up against it.

As I stood there momentarily, the silence was broken by a woman's voice, softly singing. I was unable to see her but her invisibility, coupled with the total improbability of her being there, only made the moment the more magical. Utterly entranced I waited, fearful lest the slightest movement break the spell. Her voice grew louder and more distinct as though her song, like the radar of a porpoise, was leading her to me. Right up to my face she came, so close that I was able to make out her features by the niggardly glow of the lamp: She was a woman of at least sixty-five, plying her trade. My only thought was that I had to prolong this moment, this most romantic moment, until time itself had run out. Looking me over carefully she inquired, *"Vous etes américain, non?"*

"Oui, madame," I replied.

"Vous avez pour moi un petit cochon?" I was unfamiliar with the term but her meaning was clear, her manner seductive. Stalling for time I asked, "And if I have this little pig, what then?"

"Alors, vous avez aussi, peut-être, des cigarettes? du chocolat?"

"*Ecoutez*," I countered, "my hotel room is right up the street. There I have many cigarettes."

Of course cigarettes and chocolate were the pertinent currency in transactions such as this, money having next to no value. A huge smile lit up her face as she responded, "*Oh, c'est épatant, ça! Beaucoup de cigarettes?*"

"*Oui, beaucoup.*" I had a full carton in my bag.

"*Et du chocolat?*"

"*Non, je n'ai pas de chocolat, mais bien des cigarettes.*" There followed a period of deep cogitation in which I had little trouble discerning her thoughts. These were cruelly stringent times and she had, without question, left home that evening promising her grandchildren or great-grandchildren that she would return with chocolate as well as cigarettes.

Addressing me at last with the most charming smile, she sighed, "*Quel dommage!* What a shame! Such a nice American soldier *mais*"—with the saddest of shrugs—"*pas de chocolat!*"

As she turned and the mist enveloped her I stood for a long moment remembering her eyes, a salute to a gallant woman in my heart.

I was recuperating in an army field hospital outside Bristol, England, from a "million-dollar" wound I had received in the battle of the Huertgen Forest, deep within the jaws of the Siegfried Line. The Lunts were rehearsing a new play in London, and were making it a point of duty to pay visits to all the hospitals in the British Isles to comfort and cheer the wounded.

It happened that Lynn stayed home the day my hospital turned up on their agenda so Alfred came alone. He spent three hours with me, three hours I will always prize. I was transfigured by his kindness, geniality and wit. This giving of himself kindled a fire deep

With Alfred Lunt

within that bleakness of soul which war gives rise to. By the time he took his leave I could feel my identity returning like a pulse, but not before he had given me the address of the theatre in London, insisting I come there the moment I was given leave.

They were both onstage the day I arrived, rehearsing a scene from a play called *Love in Idleness* which Terence Rattigan had written for them. Watching them work was a revelation: their style, irreverent of each other's lines, interrupting constantly and overlapping, a style that seemed so extraordinarily natural and spontaneous was worked out with the most exquisite timing and detail, as meticulously as a death defying routine on the high wire.

After Alfred left the stage, Lynn came forward to the apron and peering out into the darkness exclaimed, "Zimmie darling, what have those *bahstards* done to you?"

They were incredibly kind to me, becoming almost my surrogate parents. Every time I came to London I spent long hours antiquing with Alfred while Lynn remained in bed, dressing only in time to go to the theatre. That was her secret. She was fifty-seven, but there wasn't a line in her face.

At the time, Laurence Olivier and Ralph Richardson were performing in repertory at the New Theatre, while John Gielgud was similarly engaged at the Haymarket. As soon as I was declared ambulatory I was issued regular weekend passes which enabled me to saturate myself in the London theatre, especially the two mentioned above, all of whose productions I attended seven times.

When my return to active duty became imminent I decided that the most fitting way to spend my last night in London was to pay homage to Gielgud's *Hamlet* for the eighth time. I was accompanied by a friend from the hospital who shared my reverence for this seminal performance.

Our seats were numbers two and three from the aisle; and I had time, before the curtain rose, to note that the gentleman next to me was middle-aged, conservatively dressed and of a general deportment suggestive of a teacher or professional man who had planned and sacrificed for this pilgrimage from some distant place such as Leeds.

From the opening moments of the play Shakespeare's sovereign genius, combined with Gielgud's mastery of the role, swept one along on a wave of mystery, anticipation and awe.

With the commencement of the second scene, however, it was immediately apparent to my friend and me that we were in for a sea change; for, seated on the throne was not Leslie Banks, the usual Claudius, but a replacement concerning whom no mention had been made in the program. With strong features and a deep powerful voice, he cut an impressive figure until he rose to exit, for his height, standing, was exactly the same as it had been sitting. He possessed, in a word, a huge torso and tiny legs.

Now had we been familiar with this actor's work, as the audience undoubtedly was, or prepared for the change, we would have been immunized against the visual shock of the incident; but as it was, his unheralded epiphany, coupled with the hallowed tone of the evening, sufficed to propel my friend and me over the precipice of self-restraint.

One of the most insidious aspects of the giggle-fit is that once launched it is self-sustaining, feeding on its own corpus long after the original stimulus has worn off.

In addition, the poor devil in its clutch soon discovers to his horror that the experience, though agonizing in the extreme is, like Eve's apple, rather enjoyable, even delicious.

Assuredly its most churlish characteristic is that it is, almost without exception, indulged in at the expense of some poor soul who is innocently unaware and trying to do the best he can which, in this instance, was hardly short of superb. The last thing in the world my friend and I wanted was to mar this noteworthy occasion, either for ourselves or for the rest of the audience in whose country we were guests. Every instinct, every sense of fair play cried out for self-control and an absorption in the performance so intense that any mischievous meanderings would be given short shrift—all to no avail. A snicker escaped from me, greeted with an antiphonal response from my friend. Out of the corner of my eye I noticed my neighbor stirring slightly.

During the remainder of the act things deteriorated to the point where, at intermission, an urgent meeting of the high command was indicated. Obviously, strong counter-measures were called for. Since this was the full five-act *Hamlet* we were in for a long siege.

The campaign we decided upon called for the inside of the lower lip to be lightly engaged at all times by the upper teeth, whose pressure could be augmented as the need arose. Concurrently the eyes were to be averted, when requisite, to whichever alternate Dane was handy.

Immediately upon returning to our seats the stratagem was implemented with but variable success. On occasion, to be sure, we were able to sail through entire scenes without a mishap; at other times, however, we were less fortunate, skirting the reefs and shoals of outrageous fortune by the narrowest of margins. And so it was that our bruised bark lurched onward into the perilous waters of Act IV.

With the onset of the seventh scene we started taking on water for here, *terribile dictu*, we were confronted by Claudius and Laertes, starkly alone, with no friendly presence anywhere to welcome our fugitive gaze. A few snorts, pianissimo, ruptured the tense atmosphere, accompanied by the first blood of battle, from our strangulated lips.

Desperate attempts to right the ship ensued, followed by a second salvo, crescendo, and a third. This was too much for the man from Leeds who, up until now, had been showing his displeasure by lunging from one side of his seat to the other. Casting British reserve to the winds he cried out in a loud voice, "Oh, for God's sake, shut up!!!"

For an instant I was wafted back to my college days, when Chandler Cowles and I would go to the movies. One, or the other, would choose the quietest moment in the picture to yell out, "Take your hand off my knee!"

With all restraint evaporated, we shot up the aisle and out into the embattled London night, exploding with compulsive, uproarious, hysterical laughter.

Eight

ONCE THE WAR WITH JAPAN WAS OVER AND WORLD peace restored, I still had to languish in Europe for a year before receiving my shipping orders. During that seemingly endless period I was stationed in Lille, Brussels and finally Paris. I came to wonder if the procedure wasn't being carried out in alphabetical order!

After arriving at last in Fort Dix, New Jersey, I found myself standing in a long line that meandered through the hilly countryside. For two hours we progressed at a snail's pace until, rounding a corner, I was able to see two tables up ahead, behind each of which sat an officer. Almost every man was proceeding to the table on the left, filling out the form presented to him and affixing his signature. Since the other table was all but ignored I was about to follow suit when, at the last second, I happened to ask the officer behind me why nobody was choosing the table on the right.

"Oh, that's just for discharge," he said. "This one is for the reserve. You get to keep most of your pay."

Whoa! I said to myself. Just a little minute here! I don't care what they pay me. After five years all I want is to get out! I broke from the line, walked to the table on the right and signed my discharge papers. Little did any of us suspect that within a few short years all the others would be called back to active duty in the Korean War.

I had phoned Emily upon landing and now grabbed a cab and raced to the apartment she had rented in New York to meet my daughter Nancy. I had learned of her birth while in the hospital in England and had written suggesting the name Tania as befitting a Russian surname. With infinite tact Emily dissuaded me and ever since, Nancy, whose name perfectly defines her, has been thankful not to be taken, upon introduction, for a tea leaf reader on the midway.

Upon my return home my sister Marcia Davenport, the novelist, expressed a touching sense of gratitude for my service in the war, despite my assurances that I had merely done what millions of others had. She was determined to give a dinner party for me and invite whoever I thought might help me get started in the theatre. I gave her the names of Garson Kanin and Joshua Logan, both army friends.

Because of that dinner—Marcia's sweet gesture—my professional life began three weeks later with a splashy part as a replacement in a play by Robert Sherwood, *The Rugged Path*, directed by Gar Kanin. Portraying a reporter, I had three big scenes alone with the star, Spencer Tracy.

The Playwrights Producing Company, who presented *The Rugged Path*, offered me a contract at two hundred dollars a week. I had never dreamed of making that much money, but when I told Emily of our good fortune, she said, "Ask for three."

"I can't do that, darling," I replied. "They're offering me the opportunity of a lifetime; I can't throw it back in their teeth!"

"You're worth three," she said. "They'll think more of you for demanding it."

The hardest thing in the world for me is haggling over money. I shrink from it. That is what agents get paid for, but of course at the time I had none. Emily had a way of insisting on the very best from me and rather than play the coward, I finally relented. When I walked into the producer's office I was shaking from head to foot. "I'm really grateful for this part," I said, summoning all my courage, "but I feel I should get three hundred dollars a week."

"What! What!!!" I could almost see the flames fly out of his nostrils. "Is this the way you repay us for what we've done for you! Do you realize that every actor in town would give his soul for this part?"

"I know," I said, "and believe me, I really am grateful." I added, lying through my teeth, "It's just that I feel I'm worth three hundred."

"Well," he growled, the decibels somewhat lowered, "I must say I never expected this. We'll have to reconsider the whole matter."

I was afraid I had blown the lid off the deal, but to my enormous relief they called back, agreeing to the terms. Emily, as always, had been right.

During the run of the play the cast was called back on stage after every single performance for Tracy's "notes"—not the director's—Tracy's! He was, to be sure, no newcomer to Broadway, having starred years before in *The Last Mile* with a performance that attracted the attention of MGM. Despite his notable achievements, he aroused little respect from our cast by insisting that all the actors maintain an artificially high pitch and level of performance. When he slipped in comfortably underneath everybody else the audience would say, "He's so natural!" His notes comprised a list of those whose energy level was dropping (almost to normal!). We all knew what his game was but were helpless to do anything about it.

My scenes with him were in a restaurant at a table across which we sat facing each other. One night, as if to emphasize a point, he slid his chair about a foot upstage, leaving me at a distinct disadvantage. Determined that he was not going to get away with this I matched his move on my next line; whereupon he once again repeated the action, as did I. This childish behavior continued until we met upstage at the back of the table, both of us facing out front. At this point he rose and taking his chair with him, sat at the downstage side of the table with his back to the audience in an effort to block me. He never tried the maneuver again but it mattered little, as he tired of Broadway after a couple of months and returned to Hollywood. Since the producers had keyed their entire publicity campaign to Tracy's celebrity status, they had no choice but to close, despite the fact that we were playing to standees up to the last performance.

During the run, Gar told me he was going to Hollywood to do a picture and asked me to play the lead. To this day I could shoot myself for my stupidity and ingratitude when I recall with revulsion that, while thanking him for the offer, I said I thought it would be better for me to remain in New York to "learn my craft"!! As a result of such imbecility it would be ten years before another opportunity arose and then, ironically, it would occur through Josh Logan.

Nine

OLIVIER AND RICHARDSON, HEADLINING THE OLD Vic company, visited New York after the war. The impact upon American audiences was electrifying, spawning a vast brood of Oliviphiles, including one actor I worked with who adopted a British accent for every role thenceforth. Indeed, so abject was his worship that he threw in, at no extra charge, familiar mannerisms such as scratching his eyebrow with his little finger whether it itched or not. It took the United States but the wink of an eye to forge a reply to this Anglo-Saxon challenge; a reply from whose fertilization the American Repertory Theatre was born, out of the common womb of three extraordinary women: Eva Le Gallienne, Margaret Webster and Cheryl Crawford. Eva, one of the greatest actresses of her time, was well versed in the challenges of repertory, having launched her famous Civic Repertory Theatre on Fourteenth Street in 1926. She was a distinguished author as well and a translator of Ibsen. Her meditation on the life and art of *Eleonora Duse, The Mystic in the Theatre,* is considered a classic. Emily and I would appear together two years later in Eva's production of *Hedda Gabler.*

Margaret Webster, whom Maurice Evans had brought to New York from the Old Vic to stage his *Hamlet,* traced her theatrical heritage all the way back to Ben Webster, a contemporary of

61

With Eva LeGalliene (c) and Emily (r)

Eva LeGalliene

CORT THEATRE

Opened Tuesday, February 24, 1948*
Louis J. Singer and The American Repertory Theatre present:

HEDDA GABLER†

By Henrik Ibsen; Translated and Directed by Miss Le Gallienne; Production Supervised by Margaret Webster; Setting by Watson Barratt; Costumes by Helene Pons.

Cast of Characters
(In order of appearance)

Miss Juliana Tesman .... Marion G. Evensen
Berta .... Merle Maddern
George Tesman .... Robert Emhardt
Hedda Tesman .... Eva Le Gallienne
Mrs. Elvsted .... Emily McNair
Judge Brack .... Herbert Berghof
Eilert Lovborg .... Efrem Zimbalist, Jr.

A revival of the classic in three acts. The action takes place in the early 1890's, in the drawing-room of Tesman's Villa, located in the West End of Christiania.

Manager, EDWARD O'KEEFE
Press, MAURICE TURET
Stage Managers, THELMA CHANDLER, ANGUS CAIRNS

†First presented in New York at the Fifth Avenue Theatre with Elizabeth Robins on January 27, 1902.
*Closed March 6, 1948 (15 per..........s)

Shakespeare. Peggy, in whose presence the Bard sprang to life, would direct several plays for the ART and go on to occupy an eminent position in the American theatre as a director of plays and operas.

Cheryl Crawford had formed the Group Theatre in the wake of the Moscow Art's visit to New York, and was now about to play the same role with the American Repertory Theatre vis-à-vis the Old Vic. Her illustrious producing career would embrace works by such authors as Williams, Brecht, O'Casey and O'Hara, not to mention her splendid revival of *Porgy and Bess.*

Having been accepted into the ART on the merits of an Olivier-rendition of *Richard III,* I joined the common ranks at eighty-five dollars a week. This stipend was considered by my confreres to be a sacrifice to their "art," but I deemed it generous compared to the fifteen I was paid as a page (and mumbler) before the war.

Although my roles were anything but distinguished, merely being on the same stage with such giants as Eva and Walter Hampden and being exposed to the Elizabethan aura of Peggy Webster were exalting in the extreme. The plays I appeared in were: *Henry VIII, What Every Woman Knows, Androcles and the Lion* and *Yellow Jack,* in which I portrayed Dr. Agramonte, one of the team who conquered yellow fever. He was probably no older than forty but I spent two and a half hours at my makeup table graying my head, applying wrinkles, highlights, shadows and facial hair more suited to an over-the-hill shar-pei. Moreover, the good doctor's arthritis caused him to limp severely, a condition which the audience must have found even more bewildering!

The Famous History of the Life of King Henry VIII was our "signature" production, the one designed to ruffle the feathers of the Old Vic. We faced two problems: The first was that Shakespeare was an Englishman, giving the OV a huge head start; the second, that this play is far from the Bard's most distinguished. Victor Jory played the title role, Eva, his Katherine and Walter Hampden, the hard-pressed Cardinal Wolsey.

The second scene of the first act finds the entire court assembled while the Surveyor to the Duke of Buckingham launches into a lengthy denouncement of the Cardinal. This one speech is the entire role, and at *every single performance* the star-crossed actor portraying him stumbled into disaster somewhere during the speech. We never knew when it would strike—there was only the certainty that it would! When the dreaded moment burst upon us, thirty shoulders began shaking as, to a man, we turned away so as not to betray the snickers we were struggling to suppress—only to find ourselves caught in the steely gaze of Le Gallienne, enthroned upstage with her Henry.

William Windom and I had cause to dread another moment... the second scene of the third act. As the Earl of Surrey and the Duke of Suffolk respectively, we launched our own tirade against Wolsey. Peggy Webster staged the scene with the two of us coming at him like jackals from upstage while Hampden stood in his flowing red robes before us, his back to the audience. He was a charming man with a lively sense of mischief on stage. Whether it was his own leavening reaction to the pomposity of the occasion or not, he managed to interject a wink, a quiet obscenity or a burp at some point which, exposed as we were, demanded of us Herculean attempts at self-control.

I can still recall the smell of *Henry VIII*. Our heavy woolen Tudor costumes were stiflingly hot; although they were cleaned from time to time, they swiftly regained their telltale bouquet. On stepping inside the stage door one knew instantly what the bill for the evening was—or wasn't!

Walter Hampden was one of America's most renowned theatrical figures, as both a classical actor and impresario of his own company. He "inherited" the role of *Cyrano de Bergerac* in 1923 from Richard Mansfield (who introduced it to the United States) and quickly made it his own. Walter was hugely successful as *Cyrano*, being identified with the role for almost two decades.

In 1946, while we were hard at work at the "Old Rep," as we called it, Jose Ferrer opened on Broadway in his own brilliant portrayal of

Rostand's anonymous suitor. On Actors' Fund night Walter was invited to attend and when he entered the theatre the entire audience rose to its feet in homage to the great actor, and joined by the company on stage in rousing applause.

One afternoon while I was rehearsing a new play to be added to the repertory, Chandler Cowles, who was making faces in another production in town, entered the auditorium hastily and sat down in the front row. From his urgent beckoning I gathered he needed to speak with me and that there was no time to be lost. I shrugged my shoulders helplessly, for to ask to be excused from that company would have been tantamount to an acolyte requesting permission to step outside for a smoke during high mass. As the minutes turned to hours his gesticulations (surreptitious yet clear), with repeated references to his wristwach, grew more desperate.It was a quarter to five when the rehearsal finally came to an end and, before I knew what had happened, I was in a cab with Chandler hurtling downtown.

"Cheryl's producing this new musical," he rattled on, "Oliver Smith's doing the sets—a great book—music and lyrics by two guys called Lerner and Loewe; there's just one piece left and we can have it!"

"How much is it?" I asked, coming up for air.

"Two thousand—one each."

"But I haven't even read the script," I protested, "and I've never heard of Lerner or what's-his-name!"

"Just trust me," he insisted, "this is our big chance. We've got to sign the papers by five o'clock or it'll be gone!" These last words escaped as we dashed from the cab into Cheryl's office past a startled fellow in the waiting room. It was exactly five o'clock.

"Cheryl," I panted, "I haven't had a chance to read a word of this. Could you let me have twenty-four hours?"

Cheryl, who played life like a poker hand, eyed me coolly.

"Did you notice that man outside, when you came in?" I nodded. "He's waiting for this piece. Take it or leave it."

I turned helplessly from her tight-lipped face to the wall. A thousand dollars was almost our total savings. I simply couldn't afford to lose it, and yet... Cheryl was a top producer; this thing, whatever it was, had a better chance of being a hit than a flop; and if you never take a chance in life—in a daze, numb in body and mind, I watched the name: *Efrem Zimbalist, Jr.*, take form at the bottom of the page.

When I told Emily what I had done all she said was, "Oh darling, how could you?"

"I don't know," I answered, "it happened so fast and I'd been working hard all day—I guess I was too tired and nervous to think straight." Nothing more was said about it until one morning when I picked up the *Times* and the *Tribune* and brought them back to our apartment. In addition to rave reviews, both featured full page quote ads, blaring triumphantly at the top: 100% FOR BRIGADOON!!!

Thus emboldened, Chandler and I were in a position to act more judiciously when Herman Levin, a friend who would later produce *My Fair Lady,* announced plans for a big, brassy musical about Alaska called *Bonanza Bound*. This time we did everything right. We read the script, heard the score, met the composer and lyricist as well as the stars, and attended auditions. When we determined to invest our decision was unhurried and sober. There had been one small miscalculation, however: *Bonanza Bound* turned out not to be Broadway bound, but died a quiet death on tour from maladies judged too grave to cure. After this experience, we resolved to leave investing to others; as it was, our ship was about to change tack in an unexpected way.

Ten

THE CURTIS INSTITUTE OF MUSIC IN PHILADEL-
phia was endowed by Mary Curtis Bok, the only child of
Cyrus H. K. Curtis, publisher of *The Saturday Evening
Post* and *The Ladies' Home Journal.* Mrs. Bok, who would
add Zimbalist to her name when she married my father,
selected for its site one of the choicest spots in downtown
Philadelphia, adjacent to Rittenhouse Square. Here in rooms of subdued elegance the students, who were chosen solely by audition and
with only the most exceptional being admitted, received instruction
from the greatest virtuosi in the world. Tuition was entirely free,
thanks to interest from the original grant, as were room and board if
needed; and in the case of the younger children, academic classes
were provided.

The composition department, headed by the great Rosario Sca-
lero, boasted many fine students, preeminent among them Samuel
Barber, Gian Carlo Menotti and Leonard Bernstein. Barber, who
was the nephew of Louise Homer, could have chosen any of three
careers, being an accomplished baritone as well as a first-rate pianist.
As a prodigal youth, Menotti gave notice of being the natural heir to
Verdi and Puccini with the creation of *The Old Maid and the Thief*
and *Amelia Goes to the Ball.* Both were given performances in

Philadelphia and I was familiar with them when I received a call from an acquaintance, Edith Lutyens, inviting me to attend a presentation at Columbia University of a new opera by Menotti called *The Medium*. This work, commissioned by the Alice Ditson Fund, was nearing the end of a limited run. I was awe-struck when I saw it and called Chandler, telling him he had to come with me the next night. His reaction was as emotional as Edith's and mine. With evangelical zeal we called every producer we knew; not one person even came to look—the word *opera* was poison. With time running out, the three of us were in despair. We were so in love with this work we couldn't let go. There had to be somebody—there just had to be!

Out of this seething vortex the same idea suddenly hit all three of us in the face: If nobody else will do it why don't we? Between us there existed an abundance of ignorance with respect to producing anything, let alone an opera on Broadway, but we possessed something of infinitely greater value: a passion for this work.

The first thing we did was take an option. This wasn't difficult since we were the only ones interested. *The Medium* is a short opera, too short for an evening, but Gian Carlo informed us he was working on a curtain raiser called *The Telephone*, which he promised to have ready in a few weeks. Accordingly, when the engagement at Columbia ended we placed the haunting *Grand Guignol* set, together with the costumes, in storage until such time as they would be needed. Our intention was to transfer the entire production to a professional theatre without a single change. As it turned out we ran into a roadblock with the set, for the designer wasn't a union member. We were able to overcome this obstacle by paying a card holder for the use of his name, telling him he didn't even have to take his drawing board out of the closet.

While we waited for *The Telephone* we began to explore the possibilities of obtaining a theatre, and to consider potential financial sources. At that time the biggest "angels" were Howard and Margaret Cullman who had, reputedly, put one thousand dollars into *Life With Father*, which ran seven years, exiting with one million. Since that time they had invested heavily in many shows including most of the blockbuster musicals. Word around town was, If you could land the Cullmans all other backers would be drawn in centripetally.

For me, the hardest thing about being a producer was asking people for money; Chandler, on the other hand, found it a breeze. His main secret was to fall asleep. He never could stay awake at anything—plays, movies or concerts; invariably he drifted off and then pretended he had been awake the whole time. He was blond and very handsome, and when he would doze at a fund-raising gathering the women found him irresistible, swarming around him and cooing such things as, "Look at him. Isn't he sweet? Just like a little boy." The money would pour in; he raised more asleep than I ever did awake! As if to prove the point, when *I* explained the situation regarding *The Medium* to Margaret Cullman she all but laughed in my face.

Herman Levin had nothing in production at the time and generously lent us his company manager, a wise old down-easterner named Chandos Sweet, without whose skill and experience we never would have made it. Chandos, taciturn in the extreme, privately thought we were besotted even to consider an opera for a Broadway run, but sublimated his views in the greater interest of helping us in every way possible. We were soon persuaded, not the least by Chandos, that it was of vital importance to replace the word *opera* in all press releases with the more innocuous term *musical theatre*. He drew up a budget for the move including all the logistics and unforeseen expenses likely to be entailed.

With the libretto and score of *The Telephone* finally in hand minus the parts, which continued to trickle in right up to the last day, raising money assumed top priority. As we examined the figures

Chandos had prepared for us, we couldn't believe our eyes: The total cost of everything up to and including opening night was a mere twenty-five thousand dollars! This for a full-scale opera with orchestra and all the trimmings! Such a figure was unheard of and yet raising it proved beyond our means. Even chipping in all we could afford ourselves we were only able to come up with a little over fifteen thousand, and we needed something extra for expenses after opening.

When my second mother, Mary, founded the Curtis Institute her benevolence didn't end with writing a huge check; she supervised every detail of its establishment and operation, taking a keen interest in the lives of each and every student. The Curtis was run like a large family for which she assumed parenthood, dispensing counsel and often material help to any who were in genuine need. Her goal, however, was not merely to provide charity; it was to enrich the musical world by helping to create lives of excellence. Indeed, excellence was her cachet.

A better illustration, one among many, could not be cited than the words of Eva Le Gallienne in which she described to me her meeting with Mary, who was married at the time to Edward Bok. In the days of her Civic Repertory Company, the days of the thirties and the WPA, Eva was fighting a losing battle to keep the project afloat. Repertory theatre is not a money-making undertaking. It does not have a broad appeal, but at its best, offers something of excellence which no other form of theatre can match.

The Civic had ended a disastrous season on Fourteenth Street, its home base, and was about to depart for Philadelphia, the first stop on a road tour. Its resources depleted, the company manager said to Eva, "There is a Mrs. Bok in Philadelphia who is a great admirer of yours and would like to meet you."

Eva replied, "I have enough worries on my hands without wasting precious time on some silly society woman. Get rid of her."

"She is a great benefactor of the arts," he rejoined. "Who knows, maybe she can help you."

He persisted for some time, until Eva grudgingly said, "All right, I'll see her for fifteen minutes only and she can jolly well come backstage. I'm not going to any dinner parties."

Mary, who hadn't a proud bone in her body, came back after a performance to Eva's dressing room. After being introduced, she said simply, "Now, my dear, you need help. What can I do?"

Eva had no intention of beating around the bush, much less standing, cap in hand, waiting for a few bread crumbs to fall from the great lady's table. Accordingly, she blurted out, "I need five thousand dollars to pay for sets and costumes or there won't be another season for the Civic!"

"But what do you really need?"

Eva was speechless, not knowing what to say. Mary calmly took out her checkbook and wrote a check for twenty-five thousand dollars. "You'll have the rest," she said, "when you leave Philadelphia." All the pent-up tension, worry and emotion Eva had been suppressing for the last years boiled over and she dissolved in tears, unable to speak.

At the close of her Philadelphia run she received the second check for twenty-five thousand dollars.

Without minimizing the rest of her children in the least, Sam and Gian Carlo were Mary's "boys" and she became their partner in life. She it was who gave Gian Carlo's first two operas their showcase in Philadelphia; she it was who, throughout her life, made herself available whenever either faced a crisis; and she it was who built them a house in Mount Kisco, New York, which they named "Capricorn," with a studio and independent quarters for each on opposite ends. This was the biggest moment to date in Gian Carlo's life (and a not insignificant one in mine, either). Mary simply asked what we needed and a check was forthcoming. That was the way she did things, and the way she saved *The Medium*. This work, which has in more than a half-century been performed hundreds of times on stage, film and television all over the world, owes its life to her.

Lee Shubert, the wooden Indian as we called him, due to his chiseled mahogany countenance, was not at all the autocrat we had expected. For one thing I believe he liked us, our ingenuousness and youthful enthusiasm being in sharp contrast to what he was used to dealing with; for another, while the Shuberts' chain gave them a near sovereignty over the New York theatre, they still had to have tenants for their houses. Summer was the slowest season on Broadway with many theatres gathering dust and that was precisely when we proposed opening *The Medium*.

Under normal conditions, to obtain a theatre, a producer paid not only rent but a percentage of ticket sales as well. As we had no advance whatsoever we succeeded, with the indispensable Chan Sweet at our side, not only in obtaining the Ethel Barrymore Theatre but, for a limited time, dodging the ad valorem surcharge as well.

The excitement this project evoked was contagious, attracting many invaluable volunteers. Edith Lutyens was acquainted with a fastidious Englishman named Neville-Willing whom Chandler and I, with the cruelty of youth, christened Always Able But. He seemed to enjoy our inept joke to which he gave the lie by putting at our disposal his "flat," boasting an enormous unfurnished room. It was here that rehearsals for *The Telephone* took place.

Gian Carlo not only wrote his own libretti, he directed all his works as well. Knowing exactly the way he wished a scene to be played, his method of conveying this was to act it out for the singers. Whether it was due to years spent at the piano hunched over a sheet of manuscript, he possessed atrocious posture, shoulders rounded and back astoop. When he hopped onto the stage to illustrate a point one thought of Atlas emerging for a ten-minute break. Uninitiated singers, eager to please, would imitate his every move, causing him to fly into a rage and lecture them on proper stage carriage.

At last came the moment when our treasured secret would be a secret no more. As one final trial prior to opening we gave a preview before a wildly enthusiastic invited audience. The role of the medium herself is spectacular, vocally as well as dramatically, and Marie Powers was born to sing it. She gave the first of many bravura performances that night as indeed did the entire cast. When the adulation, interspersed with cries of "Menotti! Menotti!" finally died down, the cast remained on stage.

Maggie Teyte, the great soprano, walked up to the apron and shook Marie's hand, saying, "It was a wonderful performance! You're going to have a triumph tomorrow night."

Marie, an adamant Roman Catholic, replied, "With God's help."

Mme. Teyte, slightly flustered, said, "Of course, my dear, but in any case you'll be superb."

"I said with God's help!" Marie Powers snapped as she stomped off the stage, leaving a bewildered Maggie Teyte to ponder, no doubt, whether there was an eleventh commandment she had missed: *Thou shalt not give comfort.*

As I was leaving the theatre I passed Chandos Sweet who had seen, for the first time, the operas he so scorned. His every utterance, as I have indicated, was terse, deadpan, and articulated with a codfish accent. When I inquired how he had enjoyed the evening his response was, "Had me grippin' ma chayuh." I have tried heroically to resolve that image in my imagination, but to this day without success.

May 1, 1947, our opening, was without question the most thrilling night of my professional life. We had struggled against enormous odds with no experience and in the face of dismaying skepticism, to bring to life a work of art whose appeal, we were convinced, reached far beyond the confines of the opera house to include every single person with eyes, ears and a heart. Now it was all on the line. I stood at the back of the house watching the audience take their seats, especially those on the aisle reserved for the critics. Once the curtain went up each laugh, each sigh, each groan, each burst of applause served to confirm the faith we had invested in Gian Carlo's genius.

The Telephone, delicious meringue that it is, was dished up to perfection by Marilyn Cotlow and Frank Rogier (without stooping!). From the moment the curtain went up on *The Medium* to the moment it came down Marie Powers dominated the audience, leaving them limp at the end. No less outstanding was the enchanting Evelyn Keller, a lyric soprano of one's dreams, as she delivered the aria "Monica, Monica, dance the waltz" to herself vicariously, on behalf of the mute Toby, superbly played by Leo Coleman. I felt enormously proud of all of them and proud to be a tiny part of the effort myself. It was a night of nights, capped off by thunderous applause, shouts and whistles, with the delighted cast joined at their final bow by Gian Carlo in his favorite role.

The next morning had a sobering effect. Of the seven major newspapers in New York, only Otis Guernsey of the *Herald Tribune* and William Hawkins of the *World Telegram* gave us rave reviews. The rest varied from cool to icy. Richard Watts in the *Post* leveled the brunt of his assault at Chandler and me who were credited as producers in association with Edith Lutyens. He assailed us, two upstarts from Yale, for having misled the public by trying to cram an opera down their throats, adding that when he chose to go to a musical it was to see pretty legs and hear catchy tunes.

The effect on ticket sales was devastating. Without the padding of an advance sale, our only hope had lain in being favorably received and now that hope was dashed. With our remaining assets we took ads in those papers which had given us the most unfavorable reviews, quoting the favorable ones, to little or no avail. Sales slowed to the pace of glue at the North Pole. Chandler, Gian Carlo and I took a room at the Edison Hotel across the street from the Ethel Barrymore where, like children, we would point excitedly at the occasional passer-by who paused to read the marquee posters. There were a few who actually bought tickets and caused us to scream hysterically like fans at a soccer game but in most cases, like most window shoppers, they continued silently on their way.

With Chandler Cowles (left) and Gian Carlo Menotti (center) in front of Billboard for the Paris production of The Medium.

There were exceptions: *The Medium* induced an almost fanatic loyalty in many of its fans, one man returning seventeen times. Nor did Toscanini's attendance at a performance go unnoticed. Unfortunately, good-will and word-of-mouth failed to placate the bill collectors. Contracts with investors did provide for an overcall of ten percent but that was a mere drop in the bucket. As we lapsed more and more heavily into debt and closing looked inevitable, an event of major import came to our aid by way of heaven.

At that time, before the impact of television, magazines were at the height of their popularity and one towered head and shoulders above the rest: *Life*. It is impossible to overstate the influence of Henry Luce's top achiever on the conduct of American affairs, so when the picture magazine called to say they wanted to do a photo spread of the drowning *Medium* and *Telephone* it came as a *Life*-line indeed. The session took most of the day, while they covered all the important scenes. Upon inquiry we were told that the issue would be on the stands in three weeks. Naturally we had no way of knowing whether or not the coverage would be favorable, but took heart from the assumption that they would hardly have gone to all the trouble they did only to drive a nail in our coffin.

At this point, whatever the commercial considerations, Lee Shubert earned our undying gratitude by consenting to ride the dice with us for another three weeks. Our plight became well known, though, as we tried to beg, borrow and do everything short of steal in a do-or-die effort to stay afloat. One afternoon my dear friend Paula Laurence (who would become my daughter Stephanie's godmother) passed the theatre with William Hawkins, who had given us such a lovely review, just as Chandler emerged. Passionate devotees of *The Medium* that they both were, they were urging him to do everything possible to keep the show from closing when a complete stranger standing nearby inquired how much was needed to bridge the gap. On learning the amount he wrote a check on the spot for thirty thousand dollars, and this magnificent gesture kept our doors open for three more weeks. He remains anonymous.

The *Life* article turned out to be everything we had hoped for and *The Medium* and *The Telephone* went on to run for two hundred twelve performances. We never made a dime out of it but were able to pay back every cent we owed.

By the time the City Center added *The Medium* to its repertoire more than a year later, the opera had become world renowned, as had its composer. In his follow-up review Richard Watts, to his credit, offered a profuse apology, stating that his first analysis had been hasty and ill-advised.

Eleven

By the time *The Medium* and *The Telephone* had ended their run Gian Carlo was hard at work on what I believe was to be his greatest achievement, *The Consul*. Chandler had been living in Mount Kisco with his wife and children for some time and now I moved there with mine. What started out as a period of enormous promise darkened ominously after only a few months: My dearest wife, Emily, was diagnosed as having cancer. One morning I left for the office on top of the world; when I arrived home in the evening there was a message to call the doctor. He said it was absolutely imperative that she not be told since the knowledge would greatly hasten her end. When I asked him how in the name of God I could lie to her his answer was, "You can do it. Just kid her along. Tell her it's a low-grade infection." For two and a half years and through two operations she never knew, because she trusted me—a trust that made me feel like her most sinister betrayer. The only people I told were Mary and my father, Chandler and his wife, and Gian Carlo and Sam. Gian Carlo adored her as did everyone else, and dedicated *The Consul* to her. It made her immensely proud and happy to know that her name would appear on the score in perpetuity. Indeed her last words to me as I stood looking down on her in her hospital bed were,

My wife Emily

"Now, you just stop moping. Go on out and produce my opera." That was early in the morning. At noon they called me at the office to tell me it was over.

The Consul could never be for me the joy *The Medium* had been. Nevertheless I loved it, if possible, even more. We were all in on its birth and followed its growth like doting godparents. Evenings at

"Capricorn" usually found Sam or Gian Carlo at the piano, and we first heard the great arias and *recitativo* passages in Gian Carlo's crackling voice. Each was the other's most sedulous critic, neither tolerating anything less than the best the other was capable of. Scintillating guests abounded, making the gatherings there an intellectual feast; one imagined dropping in on Robert and Clara Schumann and finding oneself in the midst of just that kind of effervescence.

After the roller coaster ride we had been on with *The Medium* and *The Telephone,* producing *The Consul* proved to be almost routine by comparison. To begin with, in the ensuing three years Menotti had become a household name; further, Chandler and I, alone this time, had a track record; and most important, we had in our hands a masterpiece. All we could do was spoil the party and we'd have had to work fairly hard to do that.

Auditions for singers were held at the Barrymore, which would be our home once again. Gian Carlo, in whose hands resided total artistic control, did welcome input from us both; it was exhilarating to find our preferences unanimous in virtually every instance. Gian Carlo assembled an outstanding cast but of them all, the most extraordinary find was our star, Patricia Neway, whose dark soprano, imposing presence and formidable acting prowess bespoke greatness upon that bare stage. Of equal portent, as it turned out, was the audition of another singer who, sadly, was not chosen. Her young accompanist, however, displayed a musicianship so unusual that Gian Carlo wanted him somehow to play a part in the production, though it wasn't clear what that would be. Gian Carlo told him to keep himself available and several weeks later hired him as orchestral pianist. In due time, as though helpless to stem the design of destiny, Gian Carlo placed the orchestra under his baton. That was how it all started for Thomas Schippers, who went on to become one of the foremost symphonic conductors in the world.

Auditions for potential backers took place at Schirmer's, Gian Carlo's publishers. Staged by the composer with his new cast and featuring highlights from the opera, these hearings were deeply moving, as each group confirmed both by their remarks and pledges. I had invited the Cullmans and on the date Margaret chose to attend I was standing at the door as usual when it was over to thank each person for coming. She was effusive in her praise, which extended to the entire cast, the story and the music. During the following weeks, as the time drew near when all money should have been separated from its owners I heard no word from her. At last I called her and mentioned how carried away she seemed to have been at the audition. In reply she reiterated the encomiums I had heard before, even adding a few to the list. Emboldened by her unrestrained enthusiasm I spoke the hated words, "Do you feel then that you'd like to participate?"

I was shocked by her reply: "I think it would be an act of charity, don't you?"

"No," I answered, " I most certainly do not."

"Well we do," was her rejoinder. "However, Howard and I have made a great deal of money in the theatre and we feel a responsibility to put some of it back into what we consider to be worthwhile efforts; and so we're going to send you a check for five thousand dollars, as a gift." I had hoped for an investment of ten but since her confidence in *The Consul's* potential was so full of trepidation I accepted her largesse, obliged at least that she and her husband found it a "worthwhile effort"

The Consul's opening was greeted with thundering acclamation. Magda's aria, "To this we've come," Gian Carlo's magnificent tribute to the heroism of ordinary people helplessly ensnared in the quagmire of totalitarian bureaucracy, brought the house to its feet, cheering. Neway became a cult figure; the critics fell all over themselves,

The Consul: *The ad... and the producers— Chandler Cowles (left) and myself*

scrambling for words to express their praise (which they later under-scored by awarding *The Consul* the coveted New York Drama Crit-ics Circle Award); and the opera went on to win the Pulitzer Prize for 1950.

Some weeks after the opening Chandler took Christopher and Matthew, his two sons, aged six and five to see it. They were free spirits—eccentric, original and unpredictable. It seems that during the performance both developed a crush on one of the stars, Gloria Lane, whose smoky contralto and Rubensian endowments left would-be rivals begging for mercy. After the final curtain Chandler took the boys backstage, leaving them in the hallway momentarily while he went to discuss business with one of the singers in his dress-ing room. All at once the entire floor reverberated with blood-curdling shrieks, such as can only escape from the larynx of a highly exercised diva. It seems that the two boys, finding Gloria Lane's door locked, backed down the hall, turned and ran at it full tilt, bursting it open with their shoulders. Chandler arrived in time to see Gloria, who had been changing out of her wardrobe, standing just beyond the doorway, catatonic and stark naked. As he hustled the miscreants out of the room by the scruff of the neck they were screaming adamantly, "We didn't see anything, Daddy!"

With the success of *The Consul* guaranteed I limited my office commitment to one or two visits a week, all that was required to take care of current business. On one such occasion I flipped on the radio, to be greeted by the voice of Mary Margaret MacBride. Mrs. MacBride, whose words came out bathed in saliva, had an interview program and that particular morning her guest was none other than Mrs. Howard Cullman. As I joined the party I heard the following interchange: "Mrs. Cullman, you and your husband have put money into most of the big Broadway hits of recent years."

"Yes, we have."

"And now you've added *The Console* (sic) to that list."

"That's true."

"Tell me, how did you happen to invest in an opera?"

"Well, Mrs. MacBride, when you've been around the theatre as long as Howard and I have you develop a sixth sense about these things." I hardly heard her last words. All I knew was that I wanted suddenly and desperately to be home.

While I was gone during the war Emily had divided her time between "The Rafters," whose mistress she now was, and my parents' summer home in Maine where our daughter Nancy was born. Emily loved "The Rafters" from the first moment she set eyes on it and although it was showing signs of deterioration, due to lack of consistent care, did all she could alone to hold the forces of nature at bay.

At the end of the war Mary, who had come to cherish Emily as her own, gave us the most magnificent present we could have dreamed of: She completely rebuilt "The Rafters," adding on to it and modernizing all the fixtures, at the same time preserving the integrity of the old house, even to the rafters themselves, which reappeared in most of the rooms as though instrumental to their structure. For the grounds she brought in the Olmsted firm (they who had conceived and built Central Park in New York). As with everything she ever touched, the taste, quality and execution were unparalleled.

Here Emily and I spent the final three summers of our life together; and here our son was born. I wanted to name him Lawrence after her father, while she held out for Efrem after mine. I finally compromised, if that's the fitting term for a husband's capitulation, agreeing to Efrem provided his nickname be Skipper in honor of her father's rank of rear admiral. To this day he's known to friends and business associates as Skip Zimbalist though few, I think, know why.

When I left New York for "The Rafters" once *The Consul* was on its feet, I felt a deadness inside. It wasn't that I was going home to grieve for my wife; she and I had shared a beautiful Christian faith, a faith that looks forward confidently to continuing life after death. Simple logic underscored the absurdity of mourning the departure of someone who, at the very moment, was enjoying undreamt-of joy. Grief was not a part of my feelings. What I needed was to go back with my children—our children—to the matrix from which so much that was us had been forged; to think, to remember and to give thanks.

Twelve

 FOR THE FIRST SIX MONTHS OR SO MY LIFE AT "THE Rafters" was similar to that of a larva in its cocoon. I put the theatre far behind me, as the grotesque parody of a lovely melody once shared. My main activity was dispatching my two children to their far-flung schools and bringing them back in "the Packard." Emily and I had come across this noblest of cars in Armonk at a gas station, with "4 SALE" and a telephone number painted on the windshield. Its vintage was 1934 (making it fifteen years old), yet it was decrepit far beyond its years. I called the owner, Chet End, a state-o'-Mainer, who brought it to the house and took us for a hair-raising demonstration suggestive of a ride over Niagara Falls in a barrel. On our return, not a little shaken, we asked him how much he wanted for the car. "Well, I tellya," was his answer, "I was holdin' out for a slow three fifty but I'll take a fast three hundred." The automobile was a wreck but since nothing was wrong that couldn't be fixed we bought it. Emily didn't live to see it in its glory but I kept it through forty-five years and two complete restorations, finally selling it at auction in Arizona, fighting back the tears.

My father and Mary, often accompanied by Edith Braun, her closest friend who lived next door to them in Philadelphia, drove up

The Packard

to be with us most of the weekends. On one visit Edie, who was a member of the composition staff at the Curtis, asked me if I would like to study with her. Delighted to have an occupation that would enable me to be close to Nancy and Skipper I greedily accepted. Thus began my indoctrination into the mysteries of harmony and counterpoint, with weeklong prescribed exercises supervised by Edie who by now was a regular member of the weekend trinity. There is no question in my mind that these loving visits, combined with Edie's sacrificial offering of herself, kept me from turning into a troglodyte. I found the work inspiring and in time was writing short pieces, including an eight-part motet based on the one-hundred-fiftieth psalm. Whether it was through Edie's or Mary's connections I never knew, but I was overjoyed to learn that a distinguished choral group in Philadelphia had agreed to perform the motet. This ensemble gave recitals on Sunday afternoons in the large music room of a mansion in Bryn Mawr. When I learned of the date I began making preparations, which included having four new tires installed on the Packard, just in case. On special occasions where the Packard was concerned, there were always just-in-case provisos. For this two-hundred-mile trip they stipulated that two extra hours be added to the schedule as well. Thus with all contingencies covered I departed, dressed in my best "store suit" for the occasion and aflush with excitement at the prospect of hearing my first piece performed.

My exhilaration increased with every mile as the Packard and I pranced through Litchfield, New Milford and Danbury. Then, just outside the village of Brewster, the right front tire began to pound and upon inspection proved to be flat! I was flabbergasted and not a little irritated, considering my precautionary measures. Providentially I found myself within sight of a gas station which was open on a Sunday morning. Although the Packard was equipped with two spare wheels mounted in wells on each side of the car, a new inner tube was obtained in Danbury, the old one having shredded by the time I reached the station. Thus I was able to leave Brewster with the two spares intact but the delay had cost me an hour, half of my reserve time. While they were working on the tire I had managed to put up the side curtains since a light rain had begun to fall.

Continuing south on Route 202 and onto the Taconic State Parkway, I picked up the pace. The rain had been increasing steadily and was close to a downpour when, on a deserted stretch of road, the right rear tire went. With not a sign of life in either direction I had no choice but to get out the jack, a rotary-operated device provided as part of the car's original equipment. Highly annoyed, I crawled underneath in the mud, for I had pulled off the pavement, and placed the contrivance under the rear axle. As I turned the spindle and the full weight of the car began to come into play, there was a loud snap; the jack was broken beyond repair. The rain was coming down in sheets; I had no raincoat or umbrella; and my hair, face, hands and clothes were covered with mud as I started walking in search of a telephone. It took me about fifteen minutes to reach a house, where I rang the doorbell, with no response. A lighted window upstairs told me that someone was probably at home, although all knocking and ringing proved useless. Combing the grounds I found a few small stones which I threw at the upstairs window, effective enough to cause the woman inside to open it. But before I had a chance to say a word, she shouted, "Get away from here!" as she slammed it shut.

A second barrage against the window was more successful for I beat her to the punch with, "I'm not trying to get into your house. My car is broken down about a mile up the road. All I ask is that you call a service station and have them come and fix a flat tire."

"There's nobody open today," she responded. "It's Sunday."

"I know," I insisted, " but there must be some place open. I have nobody else to turn to. Won't you please try? I'll leave you alone and go back to the car and wait."

A half-hour later, to my astonishment, a repair truck pulled up and I watched as the driver, with cool efficiency, jacked up the car, removed the offending wheel, tossed it inside and replaced it with one of the spares. When I started up again I was behind schedule for the first time. Speeding along in hopes of catching at least the last few minutes of the concert, I felt like Orestes pursued by the Furies. With growing anger I turned onto the Saw Mill River Parkway and had just passed a gas station when the third tire went flat, the left rear.

(Later when the ordeal was over I found out the cause of my misfortunes: With wire wheels like the Packard's, the spokes were drawn through the rim and crimped to tighten them, leaving sharp ends exposed. These ends were routinely covered with a "boot," resembling a section of tire, which was wrapped around the rim to protect the inner tube from damage. When my new tires were installed this step had been omitted.)

While the tire was being repaired I called my parents' house in Philadelphia. The plan had been that I would come there and the three of us would drive out together to Bryn Mawr in Mary's car. Now I told them to go on ahead, there being no possibility of my joining them.

When the fourth tire, the left front, collapsed on the Henry Hudson Parkway just after I had rounded a corner, it was raining even harder. Since there was no shoulder, I was stopped in the right lane and could not be seen by those behind me. Screeching to a halt, several seized the opportunity to hurl infamies at me and my "old crate," before burning rubber as they took off again. This verbal abuse left me curiously unmoved. Any resentment I might have felt was overshadowed by the rage seething inside me at the injustice of my portion. I was quite prepared to kill, quietly and deliberately. I left the car to sit on the low cable fence between me and the Hudson River thinking, I don't care any more—I just don't care. If a police car or emergency truck happens to come along, that's their business. If not, I'm prepared to sit here all day. I'm through asking for help; it's too late for that.

As I sat there consumed with fury and disappointment an old, old, high black sedan crept up behind the Packard and came to a stop. The ancient driver leaned forward, resting his head upon the steering wheel where he remained motionless. Five minutes passed during which I took the measure of his neck, assuring myself that I could wring it like a chicken's; it was as though it had been custom-made for my grip. At length I growled: "What do you think you're doing here?"

He was not only old. He was extremely tired, and two things about his speech deserve mention: 1) There was a pause of at least twenty seconds each time he started to speak; and 2) he had a thick

Yiddish accent, almost comic in its effect, as though part of the routine of a baggy-pants vaudevillian like Willy Howard. This latter
characteristic was totally contradicted by his face, which was of sur-
passing beauty and serenity, the brow high and exalted, the eyes the
color of aquamarine.

In answer to my challenge he responded, _____ *twenty seconds*
_____ "I was tired. I thought I'd take a little rest."

A little rest! I sneered to myself. What an idiotic place to take a
rest! He'd have done better on the runway at LaGuardia!

At last, from him, _____ *thirty seconds* _____ "What
are you doing here?"

"What am I doing here? I'm not taking a rest! I'm here because
I'm stuck here! I've got a flat tire!"

_____ *one minute* _____ "Why
don't you fix it?"

(Between clenched teeth) "Because I can't fix it!! My jack broke!"

_____ *twenty seconds* _____ "You'll get off at the next exit,
turn left and there's a garage. They'll fix it for you."

"And just how do you propose I get there—on the rim? It's over a
mile away!"

_____ *forty seconds* _____ "I gotta jack—
in the trunk."

He held up his keys. I slid insolently off the fence, took them from
his outstretched hand and opened the squeaky trunk door. There was
indeed a bumper-jack inside, which I took and went to work wordlessly. Using the lug wrench I freed the remaining spare, then jacked
up the front end, removed the bolts from the wheel, tossed it onto
the back seat and replaced it with the spare. After tightening the lugs
I lowered the front end, walked back to his car, returned the jack to
the trunk and handed him his keys. All that remained was to take
the hubcap I had removed from the damaged wheel and affix it to

the spare—a matter of five seconds at the most. To seat it, a sharp rap with the fist was necessary. In doing this the impact of the blow, combined with the explosive sound it occasioned brought me, volte-face, to my senses.

I realized that this man had saved not only my day but possibly my life, by shielding me from the onrushing traffic; this man had patiently made himself available to my every need, had never overstepped the bounds of helpfulness by becoming a busybody or giving me unwanted suggestions; and this wonderful man I had treated as my worst enemy, denied him gratitude or even common courtesy. As I turned to offer him my profound apologies he was not there! His car was not there! I never heard him start up and there hadn't been time for him to leave. I raced out rashly into the middle of the road but that old, high black car was nowhere to be seen.

I did get off at the next exit and I did find the garage. The attendant started to give me a bad time about my "old heap" but I threw him the keys and told him to fix the tires. I was more than two hours late at this point, with almost two more to go, but I was determined not to turn back. Hopping a taxi I headed for Penn Station where I boarded a train for Philadelphia. Shivering and hungry, I tried to get a cup of coffee and a bite to eat but was thrown out of the dining car because of my outlandish appearance. In Philadelphia I jumped off the train at the Thirtieth Street Station, raced through the terminal to a cab and barked out my parents' address. I don't know what I thought I was doing. I had some idea of borrowing clothes from my father despite the fact that he was six inches shorter than me. At the door I was met by Ross, the butler, who had once earned my inestimable esteem for asking my wife, at the conclusion of a lobster dinner in Maine, "May I remove your carcass, Madame?"

Apparently stunned at my appearance, he blurted out, "Mr. Efrem, didn't you see your father at the station?"

"No," I replied, "I called and told them to go on ahead."

"Oh, no," he countered, "your father refused to go without you. He called a few minutes ago—he's waiting for you at the information desk."

I raced back to the Thirtieth Street Station and there was my beloved father, patiently biding his time. We jumped on the Paoli local and took a taxi from the Bryn Mawr station to the designated address, where we were met by a servant who led us to the large double doors guarding the music room. As they swung open the conductor, standing with his back to us, brought his hands down on the very first note of my motet. We heard it from beginning to end! Dumbfounded, I asked him afterwards how this miracle came to be.

He replied, "Your mother told me something of the trouble you encountered, so we put your piece at the end of the program. When you hadn't shown up we stalled for time, reading through some of the works in our library. With hope at last running out I decided, reluctantly, to go ahead with the motet, unaware that at that very moment you were walking in the door."

I smiled to myself as my thoughts raced back to that tired old man, whose materialization and dissolution flew in the teeth of all logic—my unlikely, preposterous, glorious guardian angel!

Thirteen

DURING THE FILMING OF MY FIRST PICTURE IN Hollywood, a Joseph Mankiewicz work called *House of Strangers* starring Edward G. Robinson, Susan Hayward and Richard Conte, I was watching Luther Adler perform a very emotional scene. I had tested for the film in New York and would return at the close of shooting in early 1950. A grip standing next to me as Luther tore a passion to tatters said, in an ill-disguised whisper, "Hey, is dat one o' dem New York actors?"

"Yes he is," I replied, awaiting the expected compliment.

I was unprepared for his worm's-eye appraisal: "I knew it. Dem sonsabitches never hit their mark."

The particular timbre of that kind of whisper is shared by backstage folk and the very elderly. It is rooted in the insouciant assumption that the rest of the world is either preoccupied or deaf. I was reminded of it in Philadelphia, where my father had invited me, after three years of lying fallow, to be dean of students at the Curtis under his directorship. I was having lunch with Mary and Edie at The Acorn Club, a rendezvous for Philadelphia ladies. This venerable institution occupying the nineteenth and twentieth floors of the Warwick Hotel, had its own awning on the street and its own bank of elevators which stopped only at those two floors. After finishing our lunch on the twentieth floor we entered the elevator, which would automatically descend to the street unless the operator (no push-button contraption, this) were notified otherwise. As the doors were closing two classic old Philadelphia specimens hustled aboard, and indicated that they wished the nineteenth floor. Just before the doors finished closing for the second time one of them, turning around, noticed a bench at the back of the car. Prodding her friend, at the same time indicating her discovery with an arched eyebrow, she asked in the afore-mentioned whisper, "Shall we sit down?"

"Well," rejoined her companion, "it's only one flight but I always say one should avail oneself of one's opportunities." And with that trenchant observation both sat.

With Edward G. Robinson (left) and Paul Valentine (right)

My two years in Philadelphia were a weaning period in my life, as I'm sure my parents correctly judged they might be. I had my first date, with a very attractive voice student from Salt Lake City whom I asked to have dinner with me. She consented but handed me *The Book of Mormon* which she suggested I read before the event.

I have always trusted that the best intentions of a person are acceptable to God in ways beyond our comprehension, and it makes me uncomfortable to be in the presence of an "authority" who is cocksure he has all the answers. Nonetheless I believe that God Himself came to this earth some two thousand years ago out of love for us, and for His pains was brutally murdered by the same monstrous Lilliputians He came to rescue. I further believe that those who today continue, obstinately, to ignore, deny or ridicule this fact are committing a most egregious offense. At the same time I am convinced that, while the way I have been led to deal with this reality is the right one for me, it may well be a few, or hundreds of degrees, off for another. Even heaven must be eclectic to some degree, for the heaven a rock singer might consider "cool" would be, for me, the fiery lake of hell itself. In short, if there are many mansions in the Father's house, surely there are many driveways as well. For the above-stated reasons and not out of disrespect, I left the volume unopened.

One's choice of restaurants in Philadelphia in the early fifties was circumscribed. In fact, aside from Bookbinders and a new Longchamps which had recently tested the waters, the dining rooms of a few hotels offered the only reasonable option. I had chosen the Warwick and as we took our seats I felt a stirring, an inner blush of anticipation that had been absent from my life for some time. Caught up in its charm, and hers, I asked, gaily, "Would you like a cocktail?"

Her "Uh...no, thank-you" brought me abruptly back to earth. Of course, I recalled from the caverns of my memory, they don't drink! How stupid of me! Why didn't I read her book? I was derailed for the first three courses, unable to get back on track until dessert, after which I asked if she would like a cup of coffee. When this hopeful overture met with the same lethal riposte, my *joie de vivre* wilted like burnt-up punk on the Fourth of July. Knowing I was dead meat, my concern shifted abruptly to the Havana cigar I had brought along to cap off the meal. Like a beleaguered garrison throwing up a last-minute rampart I asked, drawing the carefully selected claro from my pocket, "You don't mind if *I* smoke, do you?"

"It isn't that we mind, Mr. Zimbalist," was her response. "If you have the need to take nicotine into your system by all means gratify it. We just don't have that need."

"That's quite all right," I said, replacing the felon.

It began to weigh heavily upon me at this juncture that although the evening was in its infancy, anything I might think of in the way of amusement, a play or a movie, for instance, would surely be considered sinful. Racking my brains I therefore suggested, more from desperation than eagerness, that we take a walk, a proposal she instantly endorsed.

As poor an eating town as Philadelphia was, it was a worse walking town. Moreover, having spent five years in the infantry, putting one foot in front of the other had as much appeal to me as having a tooth pulled.

After a few blocks we found ourselves surrounded by smoke-blackened industrial buildings, with nowhere to go and nothing to say. At this point of no return I looked up from my shoelaces to behold deliverance in the form of a drunken bum. He had from long experience sized us up with unerring accuracy, for of the two he chose me to go to work on.

"Sir," he slurred, "can you hel'me outa lil bit?"

Before I could reach into my pocket she stopped me and turning to him inquired, "Just what do you need this money for?"

Now, this was no proselyte to the vocation; this was someone who had majored, interned and done graduate work in panhandling. Such a question was an insult to his professional pride. He replied, loftily, "Whadya mean, whad I nee'i' for? T'get somein t'eat!"

At this, she whipped out a notebook from her purse, scribbled some lines and tore out the page, handing it to him with: "This is the address of our temple here in Philadelphia. I want you to be there at ten o'clock tomorrow morning. I'll be on hand to see that you're given gainful employment instead of begging for money to get drunk on."

What followed was pure Shaw. Backing away and pointing his finger accusingly though unsteadily in her direction he cried,

"You're th' kinda no good son'bish that goes roun ruinin th' worl' f' people!"

Many years later I went back to Philadelphia to attend a luncheon marking the fiftieth anniversary of the Curtis. In the intervening years my date had returned to Salt Lake City where she joined the Mormon Tabernacle Choir, married a fine young man and replenished the land with bountiful increase. To my delight she was back in town to attend the celebration, looking every bit as lovely as before. I had been asked to say a few words and had nothing of consequence in mind until, seeing her, I asked if she would object to my telling her ex-classmates the story of our date. She replied, "Not in the least. I'd love to hear it, myself." Later after I took my seat again I reflected with satisfaction, over coffee and a cigar, that she seemed to have enjoyed herself thoroughly.

Finding my way back to the path of my chosen profession was not easy. Having been absent for five years, and, what with the vagaries of birth, death and migration, I found myself a stranger in my own house. Fortunately I was able to join a small summer stock company in southern New Jersey that presented an excellent bill of fare, in gorgeous surroundings, to near-empty houses. In fact on one occasion we went through the entire play with no one out front, because the management felt that two or three (or even four) might materialize before it was over. Nevertheless, this seemingly unproductive summer left its brand on my life in a most curious way. I was having dinner in a restaurant in New York with our female star, Melissa Weston, when Joshua Logan and his wife came in. It was his birthday and they had chosen this out-of-the-way bistro, sentimental to them it seemed, in which to celebrate it. During the time Josh and I spent in Paris with the army after the cessation of hostilities, we had been thrown together quite a bit. We had also shared a stateroom coming home. Having seen neither Josh nor his wife since Marcia's party I was overjoyed to run into them both, but he seemed even happier to find me.

"Tell me something," he said, "can you sing?"

"Yes, I can," I replied. I had studied voice before the war for a short time. What I didn't mention was, I hadn't sung a note in almost twenty years, during which time I had smoked heavily in three media, cigars, pipes and cigarettes.

"That's fantastic!" he said. "I wrote this part with you in mind. If you can sing it's yours."

"Well," I hesitated, "I haven't sung in quite a while."

"Never mind. Come to Harold Rome's apartment at the River House next Tuesday and we'll let him be the judge. I'm doing a new musical with him called *Fanny*. I'll send you the songs."

I arrived at the River House with grave misgivings, which proved to be prescient. Despite Harold Rome's transposition of his music to a lower key I felt, as the minutes dragged on, that I was digging a grave to my exact measurements. To my amazement, however, because of what must have been my suitability for the part of Marius, neither was ready to give up on me. Josh suggested I work with a singing coach, and as there was no hurry, try it again in a theatre in about six weeks. Through Melissa I found a wonderful character called Bert Knapp on Sixth Avenue who, like Demosthenes, believed in having his students sing through a wax impediment of his own making. I don't know whether my singing improved under his tutelage but my confidence was helped by his encouraging ways. But the hoarseness in my throat which I had hoped would disappear once I had given up smoking, failed to do so.

When Josh called again telling me to be at the theatre in three days for an audition, I said, "Josh, I've never sung before an audience. What am I supposed to do with my hands?"

"Nothing!" was his reply. "I can't stand actors who sing a love song with their hands cupped in front of them as though they were offering up two large turds. Just keep your hands down at your sides; don't worry—if you get the part we'll choreograph it for you."

The apartment house my children and I were living in had a drugstore on the ground floor owned by a benign, gentle soul named Mr. Fine. He had chosen for his partner in life a termagant who tyrannized over him and kept an iron grip on the cash register. In her presence, his obsequious toadying verified that he lived in mortal terror of offending her, while at the same time he worshipped her as his sun, around whom he happily orbited. When I dropped in that evening she was, uncharacteristically, nowhere to be seen.

"Where's Mrs. Fine?" I asked, puzzled by her absence.

"Mrs. Fine?" he repeated, with a laugh. "Mrs. Fine?...Ha-ha!... Mrs. Fine had a heart attack...ha-ha-ha-ha!...The ambulance picked her up...tee-hee-hee!...and she had two more on the way to the hospital...Ha-ha-ha!"

I didn't have time to ponder this remarkable interlude as I had far too much on my mind. To this day walking the plank would be preferable to singing a love song to two cigar embers in a dark, empty

theatre. It is a horror rivaled but not equaled by having to do a romantic scene for an audition with the bored stage manager reading
the girl's lines.

The evening before my dreaded assignation I dropped in on Mr.
Fine. "How's Mrs. Fine doing?" I asked.

"Mrs. Fine's much better. She'll probably be home in a week."

"Mr. Fine," I continued, "it was so extraordinary, the way you were
able to cope with her trouble. I was wondering—how did you manage to stay so calm?"

"Oh that!" he shrugged. "I just took a few Miltowns."

"That's an amazing coincidence!" I cried, veiling the fact that I
had suspected something of the sort. "I have a singing audition tomorrow that I'm terrified of. Do you suppose I could have some of
those?"

"Of course. What time is your audition?"

"Two o'clock."

"I tell you what:" (he handed me a small packet) "take two when
you go to bed tonight, two in the morning and two more just before
your appointment."

I thanked him profusely and proceeded to put his plan into action
at bedtime. What I had failed to tell him was that I had never in my
life taken drugs—for headache, insomnia, nerves or anything else.
As a result my system must have been unusually sensitive to such
palliatives, for the next day I had to be helped into a taxi. Arriving
backstage I fell asleep instantly, to be shaken to my senses a few minutes later and guided onstage where my head dropped forward as the
accompanist began the introductory bars to *Fanny*. At my entrance
I pried my eyes open and tried to articulate "Only you, long as I may
live, Fanny, Fa-a-nny, Fa-a-a-a-nny," but the yawns triumphed over
the words, forcing my mouth, throat and palate to expand as wide as
goal-posts.

With Louise Albritton in Concerning Miss Marlowe, *1953*

Josh (may his reward be great!) let me come back four more times. There was improvement with each effort and it was a close call, but in the end he felt, quite rightly I believe, that it would be unwise to take a chance. In the meantime I began to get calls from an agency by the name of Baum Newborn, that sent me all over town on interviews for plays, movies and television shows. So furious was the pace that within a month I found myself cast in a soap opera opposite Louise Albritton. Once settled, I received a telephone call from the agency asking me to come in and "meet the boys." Marty Baum and Abe Newborn had been stage managers who decided to pool their connections and, with two affiliates, form a theatrical agency. Upon meeting Marty I said, "I've never heard of you and I have no reason to believe you've ever heard of me. How did you happen to start calling me?"

"We did most of the casting for *Fanny*," was his answer, "and we figured that anyone who sang as badly as you but kept coming back as many times as you did had guts, if nothing else, and we wanted him for a client." Marty and I went to Hollywood together and I remained his client for fifteen years.

The role in which my natural inclination and talent fused with galactic splendor had occurred, following World War II, in *The Hasty Heart*, presented by the Berkshire Playhouse in Stockbridge, Massachusetts. Emily had starred in this one-set wartime drama by John Patrick, which took place in a ward of an overseas hospital. Playing the small part of a wounded American soldier, all I had to do upon arriving at the theatre was slip into pajamas and get into bed. I never had to put on makeup, nor did the demands of the role call for me ever to depart from my feathery nest. There are certain parts in which one feels more comfortable than in others, but any comparison with this one would be bonkers!

My second most felicitous role came along a decade later, in 1956, the year I left for Hollywood. The play was Noel Coward's *Fallen Angels*. This comedy chronicles the rage of two husbands, portrayed by William Windom and William LeMassena, toward their wives, Nancy Walker and Margaret Phillips. The bone of their contention is a charming Frenchman (played by me) whom they suspect of leading the ladies down forbidden paths.

This is a three-act play and the glamorous Gaul never makes an appearance until ten or fifteen minutes before the final curtain, even though the entire plot and most of the dialogue revolve around him. By the time he does make an entrance at the end, the audience is on the edge of their seats with expectation. Rare was the occasion that I didn't receive a huge hand which I had done nothing to earn!

For me the most attractive feature was that I didn't have to show up at the theatre until close to ten o'clock. Had I succeeded in finding a role in the first act of another play I would, I believe, have been one of the first actors in history to have appeared simultaneously in two Broadway productions.

Noel Coward's Fallen Angels. *Left to right: Nancy Walker, Margaret Phillips, and, at right, William Windom*

Fallen Angels was coproduced and directed by dear Chuck Bowden, Paula Laurence's husband. In it I was reunited with Windom whom I had met and with whom I shared a dressing room in the American Repertory Theatre. Four of us in fact dressed together, the other two being John Straub and Gene Stuckmann. Beginning with us, Windom, who was the youngest member of the company, soon gained the epithet, "Wee Willie,"

One day we had a three-hour break during the rehearsals for *Fallen Angels,* and Willie and I decided to call a dyad of girls with whom to idle the time. I tried a pair I knew who shared an apartment, without success. Willie's call, on the other hand, hit the jackpot; for little did I suspect that I was off to meet my future wife. Willie had known Stephanie the previous summer on Cape Cod where, in a precocious display of eccentricity, he had contrived to arrive at every engagement in a summer stock tour by sailboat!

Stephanie, who was polishing her boots for a fox-hunt in Connecticut the following day, had a premonition that she would be thrown. Enthralled by her and seeking even the flimsiest excuse to see her again, I bet her fifty cents she wouldn't; and lest there be any doubt, our daughter Stephanie is living proof that I always pay my debts.

"Big Stephanie," as we came to call her although she weighed no more than a fairy, was almost a child herself. It transpired that her father, Francis Spalding, was a career diplomat and that Stephanie had accompanied her parents around the globe; she spoke with a Swedish accent when I met her. This young fawn cheerfully undertook being a wife, a mother to Nancy and Skipper and in due time to her own child, "little Stephanie." In dragging her to the altar, I placed a heavy yoke on her shoulders.

My best man was Willie Windom. He loved the old, flat, silver cigarette lighters unique to Dunhill, and since his had fared poorly aboard ship I ordered him a new one with his initials engraved on it. When he opened it at the wedding he showed me that Dunhill's had, by mistake, omitted the second period, the result being: W. W Ever the iconoclast, he refused to let me take it back, insisting he preferred it that way.

Willie is one of the very, very few true eccentrics I have ever been privileged to know. Once years later in California I was picking him up for a game of tennis which he played, in those days of wooden racquets, with an old Australian square-faced model.

When he finally showed up after keeping me waiting in the car for twenty minutes I said, "Where the hell have you been?"

"I'm sorry, old thing," was his answer, "I got held up crossing mail."

"And just what is that supposed to mean?"

"I don't like to have a lot of junk turn up in my mailbox," he replied, "particularly because by paying the full price for stamps, I'm enabling them to send me stuff I don't want for practically nothing. So I cross it." The last words were tossed off as though a three-year-old could comprehend them.

"I haven't the faintest idea what you're talking about."

"Okay, let's say I get a notice in today's mail that Otto Preminger is opening a new play on Broadway, with seats available; and in the same mail I receive word from Cunard that the QE2 is offering a new cruise. I reserve the entire orchestra of Preminger's play in the name of Cunard, and the whole A deck of the QE2 in the name of Preminger and send them off. Last year I crossed about a hundred of them."

Willie had found his way to Hollywood some time after I did. His first marriage had splintered and he called me up one day to say he had found a wonderful girl he was planning to marry. When I told him how happy I was for him, he asked if I would be his best man. At the wedding he presented me with a gold cigar-cutter, engraved: EZ. Seven years had elapsed!

Fallen Angels, an early effort of Coward's, had only a hilarious second act to recommend it but at the same time, was a harbinger of the remarkable gifts which were in store for the world in the years to come. The second night of our production he came to see the play and we were all asked to remain on stage afterwards. Addressing the company he said, characteristically, " First of all I wish to thank the producers for the lavish mounting of the play. I found the direction deft and the cast uniformly excellent. Finally, I'd like to say a brief word about the author: Sitting out front tonight I distinctly counted twelve good minutes of a play, and when I reflect that, twenty-three years ago, I was able to write twelve good minutes of a play, I feel enormously gratified."

Not long afterwards, Noel was at a cocktail party which Chandler happened to attend. At the time, we were both riding around town on Vespas, Italian motor-scooters ideally designed to trump New York traffic. (So handy were they that Stephanie and I even took ours to formal dinners, she riding behind me, a-pillion, in her evening gown.) When he left the party Chandler rode down in the elevator with Noel who, upon seeing him mount the unfamiliar contraption, inquired what it was. When Chandler explained it to him he asked if he could have a ride.

"Of course," said Chandler. "Hop on. I'll drive you home."

Arriving at Noel's apartment house Chandler was brimming with excitement at the prospect of sitting down quietly with a drink and listening undisturbed as one of the most engaging figures of the time revealed his views on the world in general and the theatre in particular.

On the way up in the elevator Chandler thought he detected the slightest brush of a hand upon his trouser leg, just enough to disconcert him but vague enough to dispel any sense of alarm. Once inside the apartment, Noel seated him on the sofa while he went to the bar to fix the two drinks. Returning, he sat down next to him and this time, unmistakably, placed his hand firmly on Chandler's knee.

Chandler, who had been alive, of course, to the possibility of this happening, never dreamed it would be so sudden. Had it occurred, say, after an hour or two he could have taken his leave gracefully and the late hour would, in a sense, have been its own alarm clock. Now, the brusqueness of Noel's thrust forced him to launch into a speech which, to his own ears sounded like fifth-rate melodrama, let alone what it must be sounding like to the great sophisticate himself.

"Noel," he struggled, "I don't know what to say. I mean...I hope ...that is, the last thing in the world I want you to think is that I'm...that I'm...condemning you. You have every right to...you know...live your life any way you want to. I think so much of you, I almost wish I didn't have to—to—to disappoint you. I'm so terribly sorry, but I'm just...not...I don't do that."

Noel rose with his glass and walked to the window where he stood looking out. With his back to Chandler, he said, "What a pity! Larry Olivier's the same way."

Fourteen

My last summer in New York I received a call one day from an agent whom I had never heard of. "How would you like," she asked, "to star in a new play at the Westport Playhouse opposite Geraldine Page, directed by John C. Wilson for The Theatre Guild?"

"What do you mean, how would I like it?" was my stunned reply. "Just point me in the right direction." The only person with whose work I was not familiar was Wilson, but his most eminent name had appeared on many marquees in association with Noel Coward and the Guild.

"You just need the author's approval," she said, giving me the latter's address and phone number. "If she likes you you've got the part."

I couldn't believe my good fortune, as I straightened my tie before pushing the buzzer to an apartment somewhere in the mid-seventies. The door was opened by a middle-aged woman surrounded by six poodles that I barely avoided stumbling over, as she led me to an easy chair and handed me a script.

After scanning but a few pages my spirits which had been sky-high plunged to earth like a comet. This was a turgid piece of trash set in the days of the Roman Empire, with embarrassing anachronisms such as, "Hike up your jeans, Emp." Not wishing to waste any more time than necessary I proceeded to read aloud the lines she had indicated, waiting at the end for her to respond. When she failed to do so I glanced up to see her staring at me as if I had hopped off a flying saucer.

"I'm just studying your facial expressions," she explained.

After two or three more aborted starts she indicated that she had formed an adequate impression of me and had no reason to detain me further. Playing hopscotch once more with the poodles I made a most untidy exit. Hardly believing what my memory insisted had transpired I rode home glumly, gaining only a minimum of reassurance from the fact that the remaining auspices, at least, were still positive.

In response to my subsequent phone call the agent trilled, "She's absolutely crazy about you! It's all set. Would you mind dropping in at the Guild tomorrow at four to meet John C. Wilson?"

"Not at all," I said, choosing not to comment on the script. I was bolstered by the thought that in the wonderful hands of Geraldine Page and under the aegis of Wilson all might yet be saved.

The following afternoon, clad in my best interview attire, a dark suit and subdued necktie, I arrived at the Guild offices where I was led by a young man down a long corridor to a waiting room. When he opened the door I beheld, seated on various chairs and sofas, all the actors, at least a dozen, whom it was my lot to compete against for every part in town, and each dressed identically to me. Feeling betrayed I took my place and we all waited with the door ajar for Wilson who was yet to arrive.

Forty-five minutes transpired before a commotion down the hall heralded his advent. A sequence of stumbling, shuffling sounds brought him into view, eye-patch and all, reeling drunk and supported on the shoulders of two attendants. As they continued on their noisy way into a large conference room, we exchanged foreboding looks.

When the young man from the Guild reappeared, he announced that I was the first to be auditioned. At the same time he requested that we all remain until the last interview, at which time we would be told which of us had been chosen.

As I entered the large room with a series of French windows looking out on the street below, Wilson was slouched behind a table with a frightened, pudgy fellow seated nearby. Pointing to him he said, "Now, I've already hired this man. He's part of the cast, and so to save time I'll be directing him during the scene."

Pudge had the first speech but before he had uttered five words, the great man stopped him with, "Pick up the pace a little. Try it again."

On his second attempt he was interrupted anew at the same point with, "Now, let's talk for a minute about gestures. I don't care what you do with your hands, but I don't want them above the level of your knees. Is that clear?"

The poor wretch who had never, in his perusal of Stanislavsky, come across this particular admonition, replied most ingratiatingly, "Oh, yes, Mr. Wilson."

"All right, let's try it again." (Bear in mind that I had not yet had a chance to open my mouth, for all that it was supposed to be my reading.)

At the next sally Wilson stopped him abruptly, halfway through his speech with: "You're not listening! I told you to gesture *this* way; you're gesturing *this* way!" These idiotic comments were accompanied by a limp-wristed flapping of both arms, followed by, "Is that clear?"

"Yes, Mr. Wilson." His subdued tone suggested a growing uncertainty as to how much he really thirsted for this job.

The next sortie brought him at last to the end of his speech, by which time I had become so inured to silence I almost failed to respond. I had not uttered more than two lines, when I was stopped with, "That's fine. That gives me a good idea of what I need to know about you, you don't have to read any more."

Puzzled by a conspiracy that seemed resolved to shut me out, I stepped back into the room with my rivals. I must have registered total shock, a reaction that proved no different from the stupefaction of those who followed me. In the end, the Guildsman returned to announce that Mr. Wilson was unable to reach a decision and that we would be notified the following day.

By the time I reached home I was incensed to the point where nothing could have induced me to pursue the project. Consequently when the agent phoned asking me if I would come in the following day to "stand up next to Geraldine Page for Mr. Wilson," I shot back with, "No, I will not stand up next to Geraldine Page for Mr. Wilson or anyone else! Furthermore you should be disbarred for allowing an actress of her quality to become involved in something like this."

"On the contrary," she replied, "we feel that the connection with the Theatre Guild is very important to her career at this time."

"She doesn't need the Theatre Guild a tenth as much as they need her," I answered, "and the only thing this play can do for her career is set it back five years."

Later in the summer I learned that the Westwood Playhouse had had to replace John C. Wilson with a local man, and that during the run of the ill-fated play, the bar did more business than ever before in its history!

To get the bad taste out of my mouth I called a pal of mine, Mike Ellis, who ran the charming Bucks County Playhouse in New Hope, Pennsylvania, to ask if he had anything interesting coming up.

"I sure have," he said. "Let's discuss it."

The Fifth Season, starring Richard Whorf and Menasha Skulnik, had created quite a stir on Broadway. It is a play about the garment business with a dual set, one featuring the offices of a clothing firm and the other, the tailoring shop. The action, which is continuous, alternates between the two, one side operational and fully lit, the other in shadows with the actors frozen in the postures they were in when the lights went out.

Joseph Buloff, a graduate with Skulnik of the Yiddish Art Theatre, where he divided his time between directing and acting, had acquired the summer touring rights to *The Fifth Season*. Buloff had gained fame and fortune from creating the role of the Persian peddler in the original production of *Oklahoma!* and was now offering *The Fifth Season* as a package, in which he would direct and play the Skulnik role as well. Ordinarily Mike Ellis didn't produce packaged plays but this one had proved so successful that he decided, for once, to make an exception and offered me the Richard Whorf part.

During rehearsals Buloff barely mumbled his own lines, indicating in the sketchiest manner the business his fellow performers could expect from him. Then on opening night they met for the first time a mugging, clowning exhibitionist for whose antics they were totally unprepared. Furthermore, during my serious scenes in which he was supposed to be inconspicuous, thanks to his invidious pranks the audience was snickering and guffawing throughout. The theatre has a word for such behavior—"naughty".

Strangely enough, aside from his childish and unprofessional conduct on stage, and once removed from the trappings of his trade, he turned out to be a highly intelligent and substantive fellow. We were both living in New York and since he had no car I told him he was welcome to ride back and forth with me. During those diurnal sessions I came to learn of his most unusual life.

This was a man totally conversant with Einsteinian principles and yet he had had no education. His father was conscripted by the tsarist government in World War I, and had taken his young son along with him. The father was killed and Joseph taken prisoner by the Germans. Upon their surrender and after several years' incarceration, he was released in the port of Gdynia at the age of sixteen.

With no family or friends, he sought out the town's Yiddish theatre and was taken on as apprentice by the star of the company. According to Buloff this elderly man was a great actor; at the same time he was superstitious to the point of thralldom with respect to such taboos as whistling in one's dressing room, passing a graveyard on opening night and so forth.

Buloff had been with the company for almost a year when his mentor placed in rehearsal a play which, he told the boy privately, was the best he had ever come across. Lavishing his finest efforts on every detail of its preparation and sparing no expense along the way, he fully expected it to be his *coup de maître*.

Alas, as if to mock his fairest hopes, the reception the play received on opening night was glacial. Bad notices sealed its doom and the offering, which had given promise of being the company's greatest triumph soured instead, like milk, into curdling ruins.

Finding the great actor alone on the set a few days after the opening, young Buloff expressed his sympathy and inquired at the same time how such an untoward thing could have happened. Wordlessly the old man led him by the hand around to a position behind the set. Pointing to the angles of the flats, acute and obtuse, he stated, "This combination of angles always spells failure."

"But if that's so," Buloff suggested, "why don't you just make a few adjustments?"

The actor shook his head, sadly. "Once it's there it can't be changed. It's like a fingerprint. You can move the flats completely around, even stand them on their heads, it won't make the slightest difference."

After Gdynia, Buloff moved on to Warsaw where he joined the

Vilna troupe, because Vilnius, Lithuania, had been his native town. He married the daughter of the troupe's founder, an actress, and together they toured eastern Europe, with Buloff alternating between acting and directing.

As a result of his work on this tour he attracted the attention of Maurice Schwartz, begetter of the Yiddish Art Theatre in New York, who invited him to join that company. After a few years with Schwartz Buloff moved on to the greater American stage, while his wife stayed with the Yiddish Art Theatre. *Oklahoma!* kept him busy for three years, following which he appeared in a number of Hollywood movies. He always found time to remain involved, with his wife, in various projects for the Yiddish stage.

During this period, Buloff obtained the rights to a play about an Israelite con artist who lived at the time of the crusades. A true story, it documented the life of one Ruben, a master deceiver. This man used the crusaders' inexperience, poor communications and unfamiliarity with the terrain to sow mistrust in their leaders, while inducing uncritical acceptance of his advice. As with all great con men his groundwork was carefully thought out, his preparations painstakingly precise.

To cite an example: The crusaders found their advance stopped by a formidable and seemingly impregnable Saracen stronghold that loomed across their path. Their reconnaissance informed them, beyond the shadow of a doubt, that if they attempted to assault the castle the multilayered defense would exact a decimating toll, crippling if not annihilating the besieging force. Furthermore, this assessment was entirely corroborated by every native who was interrogated.

At this moment of indecision, Ruben makes a dramatic appearance, announcing that for a large stipend he will deliver the castle within three days. His only stipulation: The crusading army must in the interim quit the field.

The commander possessed neither the needed funds nor the authority to disburse such a huge sum, so had no recourse but to forward the matter to his superior. He, in turn, did likewise until the proposal arrived at last in the tent of the commander-in-chief. But it didn't end there. That worthy found it necessary to bring the whole matter to the attention of the pope himself who, upon due deliberation, sent off a draft for the stipulated amount.

The stage was now set. The crusading force returned and took up their positions as the commander, accompanied by Ruben, approached the great gate. Flinging it open grandiloquently, Ruben stepped aside as the crusaders quickly entered and, unopposed, took possession.

To this day it remains a point of contention whether the invaders ever did find out that the castle had been abandoned many months before.

The play was a tremendous success. The Buloffs traveled the length and breadth of South America with it, garnering enviable notices in preparation for a December opening in New York.

Rehearsals prior to that event were, aside from technical matters, mostly concerned with details since the players were thoroughly familiar with their roles. In the weeks at hand, the play was fine-tuned and polished until it shone like a gem. Any conceivable snags would be straightened out in the technical run-through and, the following night, the full dress rehearsal.

The morning of the play's opening began with a light snowfall. Nobody gave it too much thought until, around eight A.M., it had developed into a howling blizzard with swirling winds and plummeting temperature. The storm increased in severity until by late afternoon all traffic had disappeared from the streets. When the play opened that evening, over twenty inches of snow had fallen and the city was interred in a silent white shroud. Nobody came: not the public, not the critics, nobody.

The whole impact of an opening night was gone, never to be retrieved. Potential audiences never learned of the play's existence and by the time the streets were cleared, a formidable task in those days, Buloff had posted his closing notice.

The couple sat in stunned silence, unable to comprehend the malevolent onslaught that had occasioned their downfall, when Luba Buloff had a sudden thought.

"Joseph," she said, as if emerging from a nightmare, "do you remember the old man you told me about? In Gdynia, before we met? And the angles? Do you suppose he could have been right? Is it possible that's what happened to us?"

"I don't know," he answered. "What difference does it make now?"

"Joseph, go down to the theatre! Go down right away, please! I have to know!"

Leadenly, he made his way back to a place he had hoped never to see again. Turning on the work lights he threaded his way backstage until he stood, as he had so many years before as a boy, looking at the set from behind. And there before his eyes loomed the exact combination of angles, obtuse and acute, which the old actor had pointed out to him then.

"But Joseph," cried the wife upon hearing his report, "you've been given another chance! It's not too late to change all that!"

"My dear," he found himself saying, "you don't understand. The history of our play was written the day those flats took shape on the stage. You can't rewrite history. You might as well try to bring back yesterday."

Fifteen

ONE DAY JOSH LOGAN CALLED TO SAY HE WAS MAK-
ing tests in New York for a film called *Sayonara* he was
going to do for Warner Brothers.

"It's all cast," he told me, "but I want you to test for it
so those people out there can see you on film."

As a result of his footage the studio took a thirty-day
option on me, which was renewed for another thirty days. Under the
terms of the agreement I was barred from accepting work from another source but Marty Baum thought the gamble was worth it.

When a third option had almost expired and I had all but written
the whole thing off, Warner's called to say they wanted me to fly out
to the coast for "further tests."

Accordingly, I departed with Stephanie in the middle of December, 1956, leaving in the care of a governess my two children, Nancy
and Skipper—now Stephanie's as well—and our two-month-old
daughter, Stephanie II.

I tested for *Bombers B-52* on a Monday. On Wednesday I was informed that they had decided to cast, in the part, an actor already
under contract, and then I was told, late Friday night, that I was
going to be used after all and to come in Monday morning to sign a
seven-year contract! In attendance at that meeting were Steve

With Natalie Wood in Bombers B-52 *(1957)*

Trilling, Jack Warner's alter ego, Richard Whorf, the producer of *Bombers,* he who had starred on Broadway in *The Fifth Season,* and Hugh Benson, who had been my supply sergeant in the army! Hugh would later become William T. Orr's assistant in Warner's recently formed television department.

Over the weekend Stephanie and I rented a house in the Hollywood Hills, referred to as "the castle," though it looked to me only half Norman and half Mabel Normand. Stephanie returned to New York after the signing to see to canceling the children's schools, subletting the apartment, putting the furniture in storage and making all the arrangements to bring the family to California.

In the meantime as our new landlord began to get the house in shape for us, I called my sister Maria in Reno and told her I would be arriving in a week to spend Christmas with her and her children. As the days passed, the caretaker at the house phoned me at my hotel incessantly to say that a large package would be arriving which I would have to come over to sign for. At the same time my sister began to express doubts about being able to have me there because of the arrival of unexpected guests. Finally I told the caretaker he could bloody well sign for the thing himself because I had no intention of hanging around in Hollywood over Christmas, not knowing a soul, just to sign for some idiotic package I hadn't ordered in the first place!

On the twenty-fourth my sister called to say she definitely had to turn me down. So there I was on Christmas Eve in a hotel room, all alone, with no wife or children, no sister; nobody. At five o'clock the caretaker called to say the package had just arrived, and that if I came over and signed for it he wouldn't have to bother me again. Since I had nothing better to do I drove over. He met me in the driveway and led me up the steps to the front door.

It seemed that the house was unaccountably dark as I entered the hallway, but when I stepped into the living room, tears welled up as I beheld a huge, brilliantly lit Christmas tree and my wife and three children sitting underneath. Stephanie had organized the whole thing in five days!

Shortly after we were married Stephanie and I had taken a trip to Washington, DC to visit some of her family, first on our list being her maternal grandparents.

Edgar Prochnik, an impressive old gentleman who was teaching at Georgetown University, had formerly been the Austrian minister to Washington. Standing in his front hall beneath a portrait of the Emperor Franz Josef he remarked, "I began my service under His Majesty." I was struck by the resemblance of the two, even to the pork chop sidewhiskers. My imagination flew back for an instant to the gaiety of that court, and its obsession with the waltzes of a Strauss whose recent death was still a topic of lively conversation.

"I remained in my post for thirty years," he continued, "until *Anschluss*. When Hitler entered Vienna I submitted my resignation. I could not continue to serve under that man!"

Our brief visit to Stephanie's Aunt Patricia was long enough for me to meet her husband, Samuel Nakasian, who informed me he was a lawyer representing oil interests.

By the time we arrived in California, the system of seven-year actors' contracts with the studios was waning; so, for that matter, were the studios themselves, who would wake up one day to discover that they were more involved in the real-estate business than the celluloid one. Most of us under contract were paid a few hundred dollars a week at the outset, with escalating clauses kicking in each successive year. In my opinion it was a wonderful system for young actors and actresses who were rarely idle and whose careers benefited from the buildup that only the great studios could give them. (There were exceptions, of course: Richard Foran, for example, whose rich baritone was the equal in every way of Nelson Eddy's. Foran jested, on the occasion of our working together, that Warner Brothers kept him under contract for years as a threat. They would remind recalcitrant actors, he smiled, who complained excessively about their billing, dressing rooms, lines, salary or whatnot that "Dick Foran could play this part.")

For some reason, Warner's allowed fan mail to accumulate for weeks, even months, before forwarding it on to us. In my second year, one evening after work I came home to find a mountain of letters dating back as far as three months. Discouraged by the enormity of the task facing me, I extracted a large manila envelope from the pile and noted it was from Sam Nakasian, so I opened it.

Enclosed were a letter and a map. He wrote that he was representing a group that had an option on a piece of land in Paraguay. This lay between two parcels owned, respectively, by Pure Oil and Shell. Both had drilled successfully and, he noted, there was no apparent reason why the sector in question should not do at least as well. Shares were being offered at twenty thousand dollars and he estimated that if the venture came through, my investment would appreciate in value about fifteen hundred times!

A caveat at the end of the letter stated that all purchases were required to be completed by a certain date, beyond which no further bids would be accepted. A quick glance at the calendar confirmed my foreboding: The stipulated date was the very next day! The fan mail department had allowed this letter to languish in jail for two months before being released into my custody. Early next morning I called my friend and broker, Washington Dodge, in New York, and asked him to find out a.s.a.p. all he could about the deal.

(Wash had a long history of friendship with my family, ever since he and his parents had survived the *Titanic* disaster. Tragically, his father, a distinguished doctor, had died shortly after, insolvent. His mother, Ruth, became one of my mother's closest friends and a member of the bridge group that remained tightly knit over the years. When Wash reached college age, Mother put him through Yale. Upon graduating with a major in economics, he entered the financial world, gaining a seat on the New York Stock Exchange and becoming, ultimately, one of the most eminent brokers in the country.

When Mother lost her fortune in the crash of 1929, the famous Otto Kahn had been in charge of her portfolio, but Wash didn't forget her generosity. He managed, through brilliant investments, to build her meager holdings up again to a sizable percentage of their original worth. For this invaluable service there was no charge.)

After lunch I phoned Wash back and he advised me that although everything seemed on the up-and-up, I simply didn't have twenty thousand dollars to "throw away," for that was how he said I had to look at a proposition like this. Furthermore, the property being in Paraguay made him nervous, in view of government takeovers prevalent at the time in that part of the world. With this, I called Sam Nakasian to decline, and to explain the reason for my late response.

We didn't chance to speak again until a couple of years later, at which time he told me that the venture had come through, producing a vast amount of oil. Knowing Wash's judgment to have been right I had no regret, particularly since I was deriving great satisfaction from my life. But it was fun to speculate that, had I taken the plunge, I could have bought Warner Brothers! The sum involved was almost exactly that for which Jack Warner sold his stock to Seven Arts a few years later.

Following *Bombers B-52,* the casting department called, asking me to drop by and pick up a script for a new Clark Gable movie called *Band of Angels.* Upon receiving it I was told the part was that of a certain Charles. I paused in the hallway as I left to take a quick peek at the cast of characters and was dismayed to discover no Charles there. Figuring the copyist had mistakenly omitted his name from the list, I riffled through the pages several times without coming upon him at all! Really concerned now, I licked my fingers and proceeded to turn one page at a time, carefully scanning each line. About page 120, I ran headlong into him. He had ridden up at a full gallop and from his lathery horse cried, "The Yankees are coming! Gotta burn all your cotton!" That's all there was to him! He never appeared again.

I had heard stories of how, if studios wished to get rid of a contract player whom they could not legally fire, they would assign him a role so dreadful that he would beg to be released from his contract. I could only assume I had made such a terrible botch of *Bombers B-52* that Warner Bros. couldn't wait to be rid of me.

Sick at heart, I raced to the phone and called my agent, Marty Baum, drowning his hapless ears with my lamentations. Finally he said, "Go on home. I'll call you."

With Yvonne DeCarlo in Band of Angels *(1957)*

An hour or so later he phoned back to say, "There was a mistake. The role should have been that of another Charles—Charles de Marigny." Reopening the script, I found this Charles easily in the cast of characters and noted with satisfaction that he had several substantial scenes with both Gable and Yvonne de Carlo. My mind at peace, I sat down and began a more leisurely perusal of the script.

By the time I had finished I found myself wishing fervently for the first Charles! This creature was the slimiest, filthiest, most loathsome and contemptible worm that ever crawled out from under a Cajun rock. Appearing on the scene as Gable's dashing friend and crack shot of the Confederacy, he soon proceeds to take advantage of his friend's absence by raping his mulatto mistress, Yvonne de Carlo.

As if things couldn't get any worse, Gable, no marksman, returns and challenges him to a duel. Adding craven cowardice to the mix Charles begs off and at Gable's taunting, slinks away into the bayous, covered with shame, humiliation and, one presumes, lichens.

My heart was filled with dread when casting called telling me to drop by makeup and wardrobe before reporting to the set to meet the director, Raoul Walsh. Raoul escorted me to Clark's dressing room where the three of us chatted casually for five or ten minutes. My quick impression of Clark Gable was that of a private man, thoroughly professional and of exactly my height. When Raoul remarked that they would like to talk things over confidentially I stepped out, telling myself there had to be a way I could get out of playing this part!

Emerging at last, Raoul put his hand on my shoulder, saying, "I really feel terrible but Clark has this funny thing: he doesn't like to fight anybody on the screen who isn't taller than he."

Scarcely believing the good news I said, "I understand perfectly. I don't mind at all."

"No," he went on, "I wanted you for this part and you probably got your hopes up. I never dreamed we'd run into anything like this."

"I promise you I don't mind. Believe me. I'm sure it'll work out for the best."

"Well," he said, "don't worry. We'll find something good for you." And he did—a nice little part, a Union lieutenant who appears toward the end of the picture and has a harmless flirtation with Yvonne. I couldn't have been happier or more relieved.

Patrick Knowles, an excellent actor, played the dastardly Charles and came off surprisingly well, all things considered.

Under the contract system an actor had little to say about his roles. He could object, but in the end he had to comply with the studio's decision or face suspension. I never found this unreasonable, believing that a bargain is a bargain. In my first year I worked in a number of movies, not because I chose to, but because Jack Warner determined that I should.

During the fifth of these films, *Too Much, Too Soon*, with Dorothy Malone and Errol Flynn, I happened to be chatting with Dorothy in her dressing room when there was a knock on the door and in walked Mervyn Leroy. This man who had, over the decades, made such great pictures as: *Mister Roberts, Quo Vadis, Random Harvest* and *Waterloo Bridge* was a legend in Hollywood. Realizing he had something to talk over with Dorothy I excused myself and went back to the set. About twenty minutes later I was surprised and pleased to see him approaching me. I noticed he had a book under his arm as he held out his hand, saying, "Hi, I'm Mervyn Leroy."

"It's an honor to meet you, Mr. Leroy," I replied. "I'm Efrem Zimbalist."

With Dorothy Malone on the set of Too Much, Too Soon *(1958)*

"Read this," he said. " Call me and let me know what you think of it." And he was gone. Nobody had ever asked me to read a book before; up to now I had simply been handed a script by casting and told where and when to report.

I found the book, *Home Before Dark* by Eileen Bassing, so engrossing I barely slept that night. One thing puzzled me: At the end of the story the heroine leaves her evil husband and drives to Boston with a man who is clearly in love with her. At the same time she calls her banker in Boston, who is about the same age as the other man, and tells him she is coming.

When I returned the book the next day Leroy asked, "How did you like it?"

"I think it's a fascinating book," I answered. "I just have one question: Who gets the girl?"

"You do," he said. And that was how he cast me in the film. Mervyn, a man of few words, possibly because he had a slight stutter but more likely because his actions were eloquent, became one of my most cherished friends.

During a break in the filming of *Home Before Dark* Dan O'Herlihy and I were in Mervyn's dressing room when Dan glanced at his

On location in Home Before Dark *(1958) with Jean Simmons. Figure with toes akimbo is Mervyn Leroy.*

watch and said, "Mervyn, my kid brother Michael has just graduated from college in Ireland. He's arriving on the lot and would love to meet you. Could you spare him a few minutes?"

"Sure," said Mervyn. "What did he major in?"

"Set design."

"Did he bring any sketches with him?"

"I don't know. I'll ask him." Dan left and when he returned with his brother a few minutes later that young man had a large portfolio under his arm. After being introduced, Mervyn took the portfolio and spread the sketches out on the sofa. He studied them with his trained eye, picked up the phone and said, "Get me Disney." (after a pause) "Hello, Walt? Mervyn. Young man I want you to talk to. When can you see him?" (another longer pause) "Thanks, Walt."

He hung up, turned to the young man and said, "You've got an appointment with Walt Disney next Tuesday at two o'clock." Disney, who was doing an Irish picture, hired Mike O'Herlihy on the spot, and his career as a highly successful television director had been launched. Almost anyone but Mervyn would have dismissed the lad with something like, "Nice to meet you. Let me know if I can ever be of help." In Mervyn's eloquent way, he didn't talk, he just did it.

Sixteen

FOLLOWING *HOME BEFORE DARK* THE STUDIO IN-
formed me that I was to make a pilot for a television se-
ries. Especially following that film and my association
with Mervyn, who tried his best to dissuade Jack Warner,
I demurred, only to be shown a television clause in fine
print at the end of my contract. After Jack assured me he
would not leave me to rot away in a series, I went to work on the
pilot of *77 Sunset Strip*.

In one cabin scene aboard ship, the "heavy" had slugged me, knocking me over a sofa. The script called for me calmly to light a cigarette, instead of retaliating, and go out the door, pausing to give him
a warning. Here the director, not the most virile I ever met, said,
"Before you go out, throw the matches at him."

"I can't do that," I answered.

"Yes you can," he insisted. "It'll show you're really mad at him."

"Look," I tried to explain, "guys don't throw matches at guys." But
not having enough experience at that point to tell him what cliff to
jump off, I ended up doing as he asked, confident that it would all be
taken care of in the cutting room.

The problem was that he filmed the entire scene in one shot without any coverage. When Bill Orr, the head of television, saw it in the

With Edd Byrnes (left) and Barton McClain (right)
in scene from successful pilot for 77 Sunset Strip

dailies the following afternoon his uppers came unglued! He was at a loss how to get rid of the matches, since there was not another face to cut away to, not even a doorknob. He finally solved his dilemma by making a jump cut, literally snipping the incident out of the picture and splicing the film back together. It made for a particularly ungraceful blend, but it was all he could do.

When I learned that the pilot had been turned down by ABC, I was delighted. My joy was short-lived, however, for I was told that the studio intended to make another pilot, and that one, with a different script, a different director and no match heroics did sell. Thus it was that the emphasis in my line of work shifted from the large to the small screen. I have never found cause to complain. I didn't choose to make my first series but I did my second, and the rewards from both have been something I wouldn't willingly forgo.

. . .

Throughout six years of filming *77 Sunset Strip*, my co-star, Roger Smith, and I remained the best of friends. Normally we had our own shows which were shot simultaneously, a device Warner Bros. borrowed from *Maverick*. In that series they found that by alternating Jim Garner and Jack Kelly they could turn out twice the number of episodes without incurring a proportionate increase in cost. But from time to time Roger and I shared the same script, and on those occasions we experienced a peculiar dilemma.

In certain performers, whose company included Roger and me, there exists a disposition to allow the absurd to creep uninvited into an ambiance otherwise sober and mirthless. If this proclivity existed when we were absent one from the other, it increased exponentially when we found ourselves yoked in the same scene. On one occasion two factors combined to ravage our feeble but earnest efforts at self control: a writer bereft of subtlety and a director, of humor.

This was an episode about amnesia, a fact that its creator had set out with grim determination to lodge in the viewers' consciousness right at the outset, and before any less weighty particular might lay claim to their attention. In the opening scene the amnesia victim, a young woman who, it soon developed, had been in our employ in the past, was discovered in the anteroom to our offices, engaged in urgent conversation with our secretary, Suzanne. On closer observation she was heard to insist on speaking with me and I was duly summoned. Sensing her anguish, I asked her to step into my office. After Roger had joined us and everybody was comfortably settled I inquired, "Now then, what seems to be the trouble?"

To which query she replied, after the pregnant pause, "Last night I killed a man."

Poor Roger had the next line. What it wasn't, was "You what?" or even, "You killed a man!"

What it was, was: *"Last* night?"

With two words our scribe, in a headlong rush to do the amnesia thing, had managed effectively to slam the door on logic and any semblance of credibility. And the director categorically refused to allow any change whatever in the line. Roger struggled manfully against hopeless odds, but like a faulty plumbing connection, the valve which was designed to shut out "Ha-ha" while admitting *"Last* night?" became irremediably jammed, issuing a glottal hodgepodge of both. Fourteen takes later, the director's ears a rich crimson, Roger squeezed himself out of the scene by mumbling the line while tying his shoe, face averted groundward.

Every contract actor longed for a loan-out to another studio. Where his own tended to use him in secondary roles, an outside producer would hardly seek him except for a part that was worth going to bat for. Several times I had been requested for leading roles in pictures, including *Portrait in Black* and *Butterfield 8,* but in each case Warner's felt it would disrupt their production schedule. Therefore, when Columbia requested my services for a film based on James Gould Cozzens's novel *By Love Possessed,* and Marty Baum told me he was really going to fight for it, I read the book eagerly and was deeply impressed. It had great stature. This time the negotiations proceeded apace and I signed the agreement notwithstanding the price Warner's exacted: an extension of my contract with them for another seven years, and which, at that point, had only two more to run.

For the next few weeks, caught up in the euphoria of what had transpired, a reversal in my fortunes I would not have believed possible a mere month or two before, I waited impatiently for the first pages of the script to arrive. As soon as they were delivered to me I tore into them like a starving man into a side of beef (or in this case, into a can of worms).

I suppose that, like me, most actors who have approached many hundreds of scripts with hope in their hearts can tell in a few lines the quality of a work. It doesn't take very long. By the end of the first page I knew I had made a costly mistake. Nevertheless, I resolved

With Spencer Tracy on Columbia Street during the shooting of By Love Possessed *(1961)*

not to prejudge the script until I had finished reading it; after all, a great many faults can be fixed during production. By the end I knew, with despair, that behind our backs this shining novel had been eviscerated. The screenwriter had spirited the action off to soap-opera-land, that smarmy shore of pimples and problems where folks wile away the hours unburdening themselves of their guilt.

Realizing the scope of the misfortune confronting me, I went to Bill Orr, now head of production at Warner's, and asked him how I could get out of the agreement. He told me there was no way; Columbia, which intended to begin filming in a few weeks, would sue Warner's, and Warner's would have no option but to sue me. His logic was irrefutable and I wasted little time in deciding that the best thing for me was to try to help make this as good a picture as possible.

Arriving on the set I noticed, off to the side, a long refectory table surrounded by chairs and in front of each, a pad and pencil. The actors involved would sit down before every scene with John Sturges, our fine director, and literally write their lines. The original script was impossible to shoot and these efforts by John, Lana Turner, Jason Robards, Barbara Bel Geddes, Thomas Mitchell, me and others helped greatly. But we were still stuck with the basic architecture of the script and could make only cosmetic improvements.

As the weeks went on, a growing sense of indignation drove me to the point where I said to John one day, "I simply don't get it. Why do we have to spend hours every day doing this? It's not our job!"

"Don't kid yourself," was his reply. "If this picture flops who gets blamed? The writer? No, you and I get blamed. I've never had a script yet I could shoot. This is our job."

Toward the end of the film there was a short scene between Jason, my law partner, and me. Until then in the story I had been a self-confessed (soap opera) stuffed shirt, but had lately shown signs of change. In this little scene that I happened to write myself, Jason

With Lana Turner in By Love Possessed

remarked, "How come you said such-and-such on Tuesday and now you say this?"

"That was Tuesday," was my reply. "This is Friday."

"What happened in between to change your mind?"

"Wednesday and Thursday."

I rather liked the frugality and made it a point the following day to attend dailies with the producer. It was the final scene on the reel and when the lights came on he said, "That was very nice, but I think I'm going to cut your last line."

"Really?" I bristled inwardly. "Why?"

"Well, the audience knows Wednesday and Thursday come between Tuesday and Friday. We don't have to tell them."

Fortunately, John insisted on keeping the line in the picture . . . for whatever good it did!

· · ·

During the early days of *77 Sunset Strip*, I was having lunch in the commissary at Warner's when I looked up from my table to behold a blowsy, frowsy, tipsy, cigar-chewing frump descending on me. Unable to extricate myself, I was forced to listen while he informed me in hillbilly cadences that he was writing a script for me, which was giving him no end of trouble. With the arrival of my check I beat a hasty retreat, reflecting that every nut from the dark side of the moon ended up sooner or later in Hollywood.

With wife Stephanie

On the last day of shooting, and with a new episode to begin the following morning, my accoster turned up again, this time with a script which he laid on the table. Apologizing for its inadequacy, he said that once we started working together on it in the morning he was sure we could plug all the holes. Thinking he had departed from his senses, I inquired just how he envisioned the two of us working together.

"Oh," he said, "I'll be directing it."

At home that night I opened the script and, with dread, began to read. To my utter astonishment a carpet of gossamer unrolled before me, winging me to faraway climes of wonder and mystery, beckoning me to their perfumed palaces. It was still *77 Sunset Strip*, but transfigured in a way that precluded its ever settling back in its old footprints. Such was my introduction to Montgomery Pittman the writer. Montgomery Pittman the director was equally mind-boggling. For the entire week of shooting, with the exception of a few necessary moves which were not obvious, he never gave me a single piece of direction; and yet his intentions were as clear to me as if I were reading an instruction manual. This eerie phenomenon was, he later told me, equally agentive upon him, forging an unspoken dialogue between us on the set.

One other point is highly significant here, because the role of writer-director can be a troublesome one to actors. Most writers are obsessively defensive of their lines and where there is no tribunal of an independent director to mediate disagreements, filming can become, like machinery without lubrication, a difficult process. Yet Monty's first words to me were that, since he had never had much of an education, he hoped I would say my lines in whatever way seemed best to me. I replied that I wouldn't presume to change so much as a comma; every word was pure gold.

Monty, born somewhere in the farmlands of Arkansas, grew up with three passions: cigars, whiskey and the theatre. At an early age

With Montgomery Pittman

he broke away from his moorings to join a carnival, where he sold snake oil. With stars in his eyes he inevitably made his way to Broadway, haunting stage doors in the hope of meeting someone who would give him a spear to carry. Gregarious by nature, he managed to rub elbows with the famous and *soi-disant* famous, and to meet, among others, Steve Cochran, whose film career was gathering momentum at the time. Needing someone to look after his place, Cochran brought Monty to California to be his caretaker.

From the outset the Cochran whiskey began to disappear at such an alarming rate that its owner had a special compartment built for it, with iron bars reaching to the floor and a lock to which he alone had the combination. He might as well have saved his money for the strategy not only fizzled, but supplied Monty with a grand piece of business he later gave me in a 77 script where I was posing as an alcoholic. Monty simply slipped a wire coat hanger through the bars and secured it around the neck of one of the bottles. Then he lay down on the floor, from which position it was childishly simple for him to draw the business end of the bottle to his lips and enjoy, as it were, the fruit of his labors in comfort and ease.

In his free time he began frequenting the casting offices, seeking work as an extra or as a bit actor. He played a few small parts but it became increasingly apparent that he was not making a great deal of headway. He was, however, getting to know his way around the studios, so when he wrote his first script for the purpose of giving himself a larger part, he had a good idea whom to submit it to. Warner Brothers was particularly regardful of his gifts and it wasn't long before Monty came to realize that his interest in acting was giving way to a new calling. As an actor he was subject to the restrictive limitations of age, height, personality, type, culture, et cetera, while as a spinner of yarns he could give wings to his imagination and call worlds into being.

By the time Warner's ten prime-time series were in production, the producers would require writers to submit a treatment which, if accepted, would be returned with recommended changes before receiving an imprimatur; if the revised product were still unsatisfactory it would be sent back as many times as required. Monty, alone, brought in a final script only, which was received verbatim, with no suggestions and no comments. Furthermore, he directed all his own shows.

It was my unmerited good fortune that Monty liked writing for me, possibly because, with no credit due me, he saw in my person something of what he had wished for himself as an actor; something that reached fulfillment through our work together. A television series (comedies excepted) can flourish with as few as six great scripts a season, those six standouts lending a lustre that clings to the rest. Although we had a few good writers beside Monty, he was without question more responsible for the success of *77 Sunset Strip* than anyone else. Roger Smith was as appreciative of his gifts as I was and it was to Monty that Roger turned for guidance and encouragement when he wrote the first of several excellent scripts of his own.

Monty lost no time in repaying his debt (if not his bar tab) to Steve Cochran, by writing a movie script for him called *Come Next Spring*. For the role of Steve's wife, a tired and disillusioned farm woman, he was able to lure the glamorous Ann Sheridan out of retirement. Their mute daughter was played, superbly, by Monty and his wife Maurita's own child Sherry Jackson who, with Walter Brennan, Sonny Tufts and a fine cast, contributed to the making of an unforgettable picture. Hollywood was looking the other way, alas, when *Come Next Spring* was released. Hedda Hopper, who was not, chided the industry for not awarding it its due share of Oscars.

Monty had an unquenchable thirst for adventure and discovery, and took to the back roads every chance he had in search of forgotten landmarks, monuments and, especially, ghost towns, which he found irresistible.

This passion prompted him to write a script for me which was a tour de force, since for one hour I was the only person who appeared on the screen. To say that it never lagged in suspense from beginning to end is a tribute to his inexhaustible imagination and craftsmanship.

Early in the show I was knocked out by a blow from an unseen assailant. Regaining consciousness, I find myself at a ghost town, where I am directed from site to site by the malicious electronic voice of Robert Douglas. After a series of adventures I end up in a huge tank about twelve feet high, which begins rapidly to fill with water. After establishing my predicament, Monty cut the camera, turned to the crew and said disarmingly, "You know, I haven't figured out how to get him out of there. Any of you jokers got any ideas?"

Tank scene from the "Reserved for Mr. Bailey" episode of
77 Sunset Strip, *written and directed by Montgomery Pittman*

Knowing he delighted in leading people on, one by one they began to suggest an array of expedients. He considered each one with feigned seriousness and discarded them all in turn. When he'd had enough fun, he said to me, "I tell you what—you take your belt off, throw it up over your head, catch the buckle on a nail and pull yourself out."

"Monty." I protested, "do you know how many times I'd have to throw that belt up there before it caught on a nail?"

"No, no!" he said. "It has to be the first time! Any more, and they'll be on to us!" His instinct was infallible; It was over and done with before the audience had a chance to realize, much less analyze, what had happened.

While the crew was busy lighting the next scene, he motioned to me to follow him out the door. Heading down the company street we came to the last sound stage before the back lot. This was one that hadn't been used in years; as he led me through the door, cobwebs and dust slowed our entrance. Proceeding through the murky gloom we turned a corner and there before us in ghostlike wonder, uncared for and forgotten by time, loomed the very ship that Errol Flynn had sailed on in his first great success, *Captain Blood.* We felt we were standing in an abandoned cathedral.

Life never promises to be fair but it dealt Monty a particularly cruel blow in the form of a tumor on the side of his neck that grew rapidly to grapefruit-size. He had it excised but it left a gaping hole, which he covered with a kerchief.

I had met and come to know an extraordinary doctor in Mexico City who had studied cellular therapy in Switzerland. While that treatment was based on the injection of animal fetal tissue into the muscular structure, Dr. Rosete's contribution consisted of replacing the more toxic animal matter with specially prepared batches of vegetable protein. He had enjoyed some success treating cancer patients with this therapy and since Monty obstinately refused any other treatment, Roger Smith and I strongly urged him to try it.

More out of concern for us, I'm sure, than for himself, he consented and the course of injections began; Dr. Rosete pointed out that any hope of success depended on an immediate and complete cessation of smoking and drinking. Monty drank, not because he was an alcoholic, but because he loved the taste of whiskey. His drinking was never offensive; indeed, save for the very first time I met him, I never saw him drunk. Cigars, however, were another matter.

By this point he had finished a script for me but found he lacked the stamina to direct it. Being a longtime admirer of Bobby Douglas, as was I, and knowing he was seeking a directorial career, Monty insisted that Bobby be the one to replace him. At the same time he promised to be on hand to help in every way possible. The show went very smoothly, but I was aware throughout of Monty disappearing around corners, and of the aroma of cigar smoke lingering where he had been.

Maurita, his adoring wife, smothered him with care, hovering over him in the role of nurse, doctor, therapist and dispenser of vitamins. Though he loved her dearly, Monty felt that in order to concentrate on his work he had to get away, and he moved out of their house to a tiny apartment in Hollywood. Here Maurita came daily, checking for signs of drinking or smoking, making his bed, dusting, cooking, cleaning up and above all, bearing vitamins. Here the vitamin bottles accumulated until every shelf, table, niche and otherwise unoccupied surface sighed under their weight; and here, in the fullness of time, Monty died.

When the movers arrived to dispose of his few belongings, they found every vitamin bottle filled to the brim . . . with whiskey!

Seventeen

OVER THE YEARS I HAVE HAD OCCASION TO PER-
form many works written for orchestra and the spoken
voice, but my first experience causes all others to pale by
comparison. In the days of 77, I had been invited to fly
back to Philadelphia to appear at the Academy of Music
with Eugene Ormandy and the Philadelphia Orchestra in
a performance of Aaron Copeland's *A Lincoln Portrait*. This was to
be a benefit performance for the orchestra, with white tie not only
for the artists but for the audience as well.

Three weeks before the event, poor Ormandy was involved in an
automobile accident (from which, happily, he recovered). Unable to
keep the engagement, he was able to procure Leonard Bernstein as
a replacement, and the performance went ahead as scheduled.

A Lincoln Portrait is not my favorite work. For one thing, it re-
quires the narrator (Mr. Interlocutor, me) to stand, rather than remain seated, during an interminable opening orchestral interlude.
So there I am, one penguin among many, staring out upon a sea of
penguins, Philadelphia's choicest and rarest, whose checkbooks have
made the evening possible. He (LB) is conducting away furiously,
hair flying, while I with nothing to do am trying to figure out where
to put my face.

All the way across the proscenium, from one side to the other, is draped a heavy velvet shroud along the length of which microphones are affixed at regular intervals, although I am only dimly aware of it as I stand there attempting an expression to conceal that I wish I could be elsewhere. All at once, as suddenly as disaster must have overtaken the citizens of Pompeii, there is a blur of red as the whole contrivance comes crashing to the floor, microphones and all. Monocles pop, lorgnettes fly from bosoms and the sucking sound of air being gulped in fills the hall. Since all this occurs during a fortissimo passage, he (LB) is oblivious to it as his hair reaches hurricane proportions.

Before I have a chance to collect myself he throws me a cue and I start to speak. The only way I can describe what emerges from my lips is to compare it to the sound of Marcel Marceau. Bernstein is totally unaware of anything being amiss as I persevere to the end, a figure without hope. I can plainly see eyes closing and silver heads flopping onto brocaded shoulders. I can't even hear what I am saying myself; in that immense hall an orchestra is tootling away while some fellow from Hollywood is doing facial exercises.

When we come to the last note there is a deafening silence. We (he and I) slink off the stage like whipped dogs, he still oblivious to what has happened. Bernstein, like many comics, has a support group, trained to greet his exits with "Fantastic, Lenny!" or "You were unbelievable tonight!" On this occasion, it's "Lenny, a f---in' disaster!!!"

"Wha...wha...what?"

On hearing the reason for their consternation he yanks me after him like a kite and flies back on stage. "Folks!" he cries, waving his arms, "Folks!!" The startled penguins, who have never been so addressed, look about bleakly. "Folks, we're terribly sorry for what happened tonight. Tell you what, all those who'd like to hear it over again, raise your hands." He is greeted by an icy wall of disdain. We wait. And we wait. After what seems like an aeon, one hand is raised to half-mast followed, from across the auditorium, by another. The wall is cracked. Soon hands begin sprouting up everywhere until at last, like a chrysalis, the thing not to do is transmuted into the thing to do.

"You're on!" cries LB and, as soon as a few microphones are hurriedly assembled, we launch into a reprise, this time greeted with thunderous acclamation.

The last year of *77 Sunset Strip* Jack Warner fired the entire television department, including all the regulars in our cast except me. He brought in Jack Webb to head television operations and Bill Conrad to be our producer. Where there had been fifty–odd actors under contract, I was now the only one left. The format of our show was completely changed and my character transformed into a civilian Sergeant Friday, even to the slacks and sport jacket identified with Webb in *Dragnet*. As might have been expected, the effect on our ratings was catastrophic. Some viewers kept switching channels, searching desperately for the familiar trappings of the old show; others simply couldn't understand what disaster had overtaken one of their favorite programs.

Despite such an enormous miscalculation on the front office's part, thanks to Bill Conrad's creativity we were able that year to turn out some memorable episodes. Chief among them was a five-part story, a kind of series within a series, which he directed himself, that featured twenty-four guest stars, including Leonid Kinsky, the great Russian actor, whose comedic gifts had graced innumerable films. Mostly these guest performers were called upon to play *vignettes*, and Kinsky's required merely a half-day's work. He was to portray an art

A five-part 77 Sunset Strip *story, with 24 guest stars*

instructor to a group of silly and ungifted suburban ladies, in a scene that consisted of his moving from one canvas to the next making flattering comments—in order to retain his job—while registering, privately, his revulsion at their offerings.

The morning he was to report for work Kinsky phoned Bill Conrad asking to be allowed to come in a half-hour late.

"Sure," said Bill. "What's the problem?"

"Last night," he replied, "my brother was killed in a car accident in Florida."

"I'm so sorry, Lenny," said Bill.

"And this morning, at five o'clock, my wife died from a heart attack." I had worked with his wife, a most beautiful woman, and knew how deeply in love they both were.

"Oh, Lenny," Bill sighed, "we're going to be here for weeks on this show. You just call me and tell me when you're ready to come in. We can do the scene any time. Don't have it on your mind now."

"No, I want to come in this morning. All I need is an extra half-hour."

"You've got it," was Bill's reply.

Kinsky arrived on the minute and, after he had been made up and decked out in a floppy beret and smock, we began rehearsals. I don't recall why I was in the scene at all; it was entirely his. He had a lot of dialogue, pages of it, and on the first take he made it through at least a page before "going up" in his lines. He was so funny that, standing next to him, I had to turn away to keep from laughing.

With the camera cut in preparation for a pickup, his eyes filled with tears and as the makeup man dried his face, he apologized to me! He only required three more takes, each funnier than the last, each interim marked by more tears and an apology.

When it was over and he retired to his dressing room, we moved on to another set and the next scene. Emerging at last, he said good-bye and thanked Bill before heading for the door that led to the street. He never made it through. All the rest of the day he stood there, watching us until the very last take. He had no more home to go to; we were the closest thing to it he had left.

From time to time in those days, we used to have dinner at a health-food restaurant on the Strip called The Aware Inn. To my knowledge it was one of the first of its kind in the country. It was small and, more to the point, narrow, with the maximum number of tables possible crowded together along the walls. The young and sprightly headwaiter was always very kind to me, and delighted in introducing me to people he thought might be helpful in my work.

One evening I had taken my son, Skipper, there to dinner, where we were shoehorned into our seats by the aforementioned *maître d'hôtel,* Jay. From the outset I noticed that he was unusually excited, racing hither and yon in a flurry of activity. In one hurried pass by our table he dropped off a note which read, "Don't turn around now, but the person with her back to you is Greta Garbo."

We were seated in straight-backed chairs with but two narrow dorsal supports, and because we were jammed in like sardines, I could distinctly feel her back against mine. By the time the entrée rolled around, Jay paused long enough to whisper that he had arranged with one of his friends at a table behind me to let me pretend to have a conversation with him, so that as I returned to my own table I could get a good look at Garbo's face.

I thanked Jay, telling him I didn't think it was the time for that to happen. What I saw no need to mention was that, without even moving and totally within the bounds of propriety, I had something far more precious: The face I would have seen might have borne the scars of six decades of disenchantment, whereas the back that was mine was the back of Mata Hari, and of Camille and of Queen Christina.

Skipper was home on vacation from boarding school at the time of the above incident. He spent four years at the Robert Louis Stevenson School in Pebble Beach, California, on whose board he served in later years.

For Christmas, Easter and summer holidays he would fly home to Los Angeles and I would meet his plane. On one occasion, however, I saw no sign of him among the passengers coming through the gate; a search of the terminal yielded no clue to his whereabouts. Greatly worried, I went to the courtesy telephone, gave his full name and mine and requested that he be told to join me at the baggage carousel. Meanwhile, I stepped up my efforts, flying from gate to baggage to every conceivable location in between. When a message blared forth on the loudspeaker, "Mr. Zinzibar, please report to the white courtesy telephone," being almost frantic by now I paid little heed. A second salvo followed: "Mr. Zinzibar, please report to the white courtesy telephone. Mr. Ezra Zinzibar!"

At least a minute later it hit me! Skidding to a stop, I reversed my tracks and raced to the white telephone. "My name is Efrem Zimbalist, E-f-r-e-m Z-i-m-b-a-l-i-s-t," I managed to gulp out. "I left word for my son, who has the same name, to meet me at baggage. Just now I heard Ezra Zinzibar paged and told to report to this telephone. I'm sure that must have been intended for me."

"No, Mr. Zimbalist," was the reply, "I have your message in front of me. I was paging Mr. Ezra Zinzibar!"

· · ·

If I were to be asked which of all my experiences in Hollywood I found the most enjoyable, I would respond without hesitation: working on my daughter's series, *Remington Steele*. Turning up on her set, in contrast to my own, was a source of pleasure and pride only a parent can know.

In one instance it was also the occasion of unwelcome, yet uncontrollable mirth. We had a scene together, involving a lot of dialogue, which called for us to be dancing around the living room. Movie dancing, if one is not Fred Astaire or Ginger Rogers, is a rather sim-

With Pierce Brosnan and Stephanie in Remington Steele

*With daughter Stephanie in the famous
dancing scene of a* Remington Steele *episode*

ple affair: the long shot, showing the entire body, as well as any number of other bodies, is employed to establish the surroundings, and
not to eavesdrop on the conversation of the dancers. To focus on
what they are saying, the camera moves in to a waist shot or closer,
which renders what the feet are doing irrelevant. Beyond a slight
swaying motion, all that is required is that the face of the one doing
the talking be turned in the general direction of the camera.

For our scene that day the powers on high had, unaccountably,
engaged the services of a dancing master, who must have nosed an
opportunity to become the Baryshnikov of episodic television.
Stephanie and I arrived on the set to find ourselves the victims of a
fait accompli: our stand-ins were twirling around sofas and tables to

the recorded strains of a full orchestra, with the tyrant of the toe in total command. Instead of a conversation between two people who happened to be dancing, under his baton it had metamorphosed into a galop punctuated by chattering.

As Stephanie and I assumed the positions vacated by our stand-ins, we were notified that the sound department required a clean track upon which to record our lines. There would have to be complete silence on the set; the music would be dubbed in later during editing. Recognizing that our feet would need to move in unison due to the complex routine we were about to attempt, "sound" placed tiny devices in our ears which blared out the music we alone could hear.

Unfortunately, what we could not hear was what the other was saying or, for that matter, what we ourselves were saying. To deal with this absurd situation, we were thrown back on lip-reading, which presented us with a worse dilemma: Since we could hear nothing but the music, the beat, in pat-head-rub-tummy fashion, so impregnated our dialogue that it came out something like: "What IS your INterest IN my MOTHer?"

"I SIMply THINK she's A verY fine LAdy."

With the insistent "AND a one AND a two" of the dancing master adding to the mix, Stephanie and I broke down completely and rolled on the floor with irrepressible laughter. It took makeup almost an hour to repair the damage, after which we knocked out the scene in short order as it should have been done in the first place, sans Baryshnikov.

I am not, in fact, much of a dancer; dancing has never been of particular interest to me, beyond the pleasure of holding a girl in my arms while swaying to the lilt of non-obtrusive music. Today's exhibitionism, adoring of self rather than self's partner . . . indulged in to the jangle of percussive excrescences is, in the words of Cole Porter, "my idea of nothing to do."

What little I know about dancing was gleaned from "coming-out" parties in the thirties, where all one was required to bring to the table were tails, a silk or opera hat, a corsage and a basic competency in the foxtrot, waltz and polka. With these simple skills I was able to survive for two decades, mainly because marriage and the manly art of war kept me off the dance floor.

Emerging from self-exile in the fifties following the loss of my wife, I found myself back in the dreary world of dating and, perforce, dancing. The intervening years had raised the bar with the craze for Latin dances, which I knew nothing at all about, beyond a vague familiarity with the lingual and corporal exertions of Carmen Miranda.

To meet this threat, the strategy I devised was three pronged: at the first hint of a marimba or bongo drum I would wiggle for a bar or two before escorting my date, resolutely, to the table. This move admitted no weakness, while implying a later return to the arena that I was careful to time with what I hoped would continue to be a foxtrot interlude. In the event of a renewed attack from south-of-the-border before we had left the floor, two options still remained: the first was to suggest a drink. In the unlucky event of a third crisis, I would remark that the girl looked a little peaked—a ruse that usually enlisted her own cooperation in returning to the table.

Over time, all these deceptions proved wearing on my nervous system to the point where it became clear that in order to survive, I simply had to learn the hated dances. I called Arthur Murray and signed up for a course of twenty lessons.

Upon arriving at the studio I was directed to a hermetically sealed cell within whose glass walls my proctoress, a perpetual sucker of mint drops, awaited me. To the Muzak imperative of a trumpet ensemble my first hour began, in which I was taught to emulate the spaghetti movements of the mambo. In that longest hour of my life, not because of my teacher who was excellent but because I was doing what I dearly loathed, I managed to learn only three or four steps before the bell, which I had been waiting an eternity to hear, signaled freedom.

Once out on the street, I doubted I could endure any more such experiences and seriously considered ducking the remainder of my lessons, although they had been paid for in advance. Reason (and thrift) prevailed and I went on to learn extended routines in the rumba, samba and tango as well.

My heart was light as, eighteen lessons and a dozen packets of Crysto-mints later, I approached the studio for my final session. Upon entering my glass box, I was disconcerted to see a woman seated inside the door with a clipboard on her lap; worse still, she showed no inclination to leave once we began. Merely to survive the rigors of a dancing lesson was bad enough; to be scrutinized doing it was insufferable. Except to jot down an occasional note, the woman never took her eyes off me once.

When that reluctant bell rang at last, I bolted for the door and deliverance, only to be stopped by: "Mr. Zimbalist, you have the potential to be one of the truly great dancers in New York. If you would sign up for, say, another fifty lessons..."

I was out of the building before she could finish the conditional.

En route from the table to the dance floor that same night, having waited for a samba, I was itching to show off my routines. It was a disaster! My date stumbled all over my feet and I over hers. A subsequent occasion proved equally calamitous, as did several more. The problem, I learned eventually, was that nobody knew my sequences. The entire effort and time I had so wearisomely invested had been for nothing.

After all my dutiful obeisances at the feet of Terpsichore I ended up exactly where I had begun, with: "Let's have something to drink." and, "You look a little peaked."

Eighteen

 Several months before filming began on *The FBI* series, I was brought back to Washington in order to become acquainted, at least superficially, with the general activity of the Bureau and to interview Mr. Hoover and the heads of the various divisions. It was on this occasion that I met Cartha D. DeLoach, Hoover's associate director on whom he leaned heavily. DeLoach, known to friends as Deke, was the Bureau's liaison to the Johnson White House as well as to General Westmoreland's headquarters in Vietnam; at the same time he was to represent the FBI's interests in our television series. When I poked my head into his office for the first time he was talking simultaneously with Johnson and Westmoreland. Concurrently he managed to listen with his third ear to one Sam Clark, Warner Brothers' merchandising emissary, who was seeking the Bureau's consent to the hawking of FBI T-shirts!

During my visit, Deke asked me if my wife and I would like an invitation to dinner at the White House. I replied that, although we would be greatly honored, I as a conservative Republican would probably not be welcome. "Oh," he said, "that's of no importance. My secretary will make the arrangements."

In due time we received notice from the White House that a

In the Johnsons' receiving line with Stephanie

formal invitation would be forthcoming. A few weeks later the engraved invitation itself arrived, for dinner in honor of the Shah of Iran. This was subsequently annulled by a telegram which announced that, due to unforeseen circumstances, the Shah's presence was required in Iran. The unforeseen circumstances proved to be the Israeli war against Egypt and Syria. Feeling that a little piece of history had dropped into our laps, I had the three communications mounted, sequentially, in a frame.

Later, a new invitation arrived with the president of Chad as the guest of honor. At a White House dinner, the order of protocol calls for the husband to precede his wife through the receiving line. It did come as somewhat of a shock to me as I shook President Johnson's hand to have him accompany his words of greeting with a decided wink. Feeling more at ease after this, I watched Stephanie receive the same token of intimacy, as he informed her that they would be seeing more of each other later on. He was alluding to the fact that she would be sitting at his table. At large dinners it is the custom for the guests to be seated at separate tables spread throughout the room. As we observed others following us through the line, it became obvious that each was the beneficiary of a wink; this supposed mark of confidentiality was nothing more than a muscular tic, involuntary and impartial!

We were told that the president had had a particularly difficult and exhausting day. The chieftain of Chad did little to improve it. Instead, he took advantage of his role as guest to lacerate the United States in general and Johnson in particular for not giving his country enough money; there was not a word of thanks for all the aid it had received. During this ungracious tirade Johnson's head slumped forward and he seemed to be falling asleep. Afterwards I learned from other members of his table that it was my wife who succeeded in rescuing him from his despondency.

Stephanie was placed on earth, I suspect, with a special dispensation in mind: to be the friend, nurturer and protector of the entire animal kingdom, and with enough benevolence left over to extend, somewhat, to the human race as well. Many were the mosquitoes I watched being tenderly borne out our front door by the wings, and set free to pursue their depredations upon a new host of two-legged victims. Our homestead could most aptly be described as an ark, with a few modest quarters for the attendants.

Since Johnson's passion was his ranch, it wasn't long before the two of them had hit it off famously, turning with gusto from the plaints of Chad to the stall-mucking, hog-slopping world dear to both of them. His color returned, his eyes lit up and when he left for the night, there was a bounce to his step.

· · ·

At a point in his career when he was Special Agent in Charge of the Cleveland office (there are no agents in the FBI who are not special), Deke received an urgent call from a man who identified himself as Maurice Gusman. With the exception of bank robbery, the only theft over which the FBI has jurisdiction is interstate theft; what Deke's caller reported was definitely that—an entire railroad car had been hijacked. What made this noteworthy for the FBI was that its payload was condoms! Deke was able to retrieve the precious cargo and, as a result, the two men developed a liking for each other which in time ripened into a deep friendship.

Through Deke I met Maurice Gusman and came to know his unique history. By that time he was in his late eighties. His American experience had begun when, as a boy of seven, he arrived unescorted from Russia. Placed in quarantine on Ellis Island, the tiny immigrant who spoke no English was eventually released to make his way to Brooklyn and his only contact, an uncle he had never met. The uncle owned a drugstore and generously gave the boy a job as gofer and mopster. Gus was intensely industrious, working and studying with vigor, and determined one day to repay the debt he owed his befriender and the country that had adopted him.

In time his uncle made him full partner and bequeathed the store to him on his death. Before long, Gus had expanded the enterprise into a chain of drugstores, which led him ultimately into the wholesale drug business. He amassed an enormous fortune that allowed him to endow Florida State, among many other beneficiaries of his philanthropy, with a magnificent concert hall which bears his name.

Although small in stature, Gus, who sported a military moustache, was neatly groomed and extremely well dressed. In his nineties he was an outrageous flirt teeming with continental charm, a threat to any woman in the same county, however loftily she might tower over him. What made him equally attractive to both sexes was a

Maurice Gusman

brightness of personality, a keen interest in the preoccupations of those around him and a contagious optimism.

I had not known him very long before it became apparent that he viewed his life as a balance sheet. The credits were his formidable achievements; the debit, the obligation he felt toward the country that had opened its arms to a homeless immigrant boy and placed those achievements within his reach. I'll never forget the graphic illustration of that sentiment I experienced the first time I visited him in Miami where he lived. We had been chatting in his office, perched high above the city in a building that was the cornerstone of his empire, when he jumped up and motioned to me to follow him out the door and down the hall. Entering a small cubicle, I beheld a safe, approximately four feet wide by six feet tall which, when he swung the door open, proved to be jammed to overflowing with stock certificates.

"Gus," I exclaimed, "I didn't know you played the market!"

"I don't *play* the market," he corrected me with emphasis. "I've never sold one share of stock and never will. This represents the portion of our great country that has been entrusted to my care. It's not negotiable."

Towards the end of his life, Gus sent me his autobiography which he had had ghostwritten. Here again one encountered the ever-recurrent theme of his passion to repay this country for its blessings, and his despair that he might never be given the chance.

Then out of the blue, that which he had awaited for more than eighty years came to pass: An invitation was extended to him by President Johnson to head a trade mission to one of the African countries. He would hold the temporary rank of full ambassador, but there would be no salary. His prayers answered, Gus threw himself into the task, bringing all his business acumen and organizational ability into play. Thanks to his efforts the affair was a resounding success, up to the last dot of the final report which he submitted to the White House.

In his book, he recorded his joy at receiving a letter of appreciation and commendation from the president. This, however, was soon outshone by an invitation to dinner at the White House.

"But my greatest thrill of all," he wrote, "greater than the letter and greater than the invitation itself came when, as I shook the President's hand, he winked at me."

When Gus died, the books finally balanced.

My initial visit to FBI headquarters was climaxed, on the final day, by an interview with Mr. Hoover. My day-by-day schedule had been carefully plotted, with every half-hour accounted for. Only once did the wheels come off, when I stepped into the elevator one afternoon to find myself alone, face to face, with the director himself. We both averted our eyes, as if by so doing the event would be invalidated, and proceeded wordlessly to our destinations.

Three days later when the interview took place, no mention was made of the incident. Deke accompanied me into the historic office and sat beside me as the talk began.

Almost everything about J. Edgar Hoover surprised me. He was taller than I expected—a good six feet. His speech, which betrayed the hint of a soft, Southern lilt, was courtly yet congenial. A formal man, he dominated the conversation with an easy, unfaltering flow of words, to such an extent that it was impossible to interpose even the niceties, "I see," or "Oh, yes." This interdiction of repartee, far from offending, afforded one a box seat, as it were, from which to contemplate the fascinating span of his life without the necessity of holding up one's end.

Like a seagull in flight, dipping occasionally to investigate something of interest in the ocean, his attention would focus momentarily on disparate subjects, such as Mrs. McLean and the Hope diamond, Martin Luther King, Jr., Hollywood, Washington society, Khrushchev and Shirley Temple, and then pass on. It was a virtuoso performance, allegro con brio, and he never paused for a word.

When we rose at last and stepped outside for a quick shot from the FBI photographer, I glanced at my watch for the first time and noted, with disbelief, that we were two hours and four minutes older.

A week later a note arrived telling me how much he had enjoyed our time together. It was brief, as were the many that were to follow over the years, yet it contained a surprise: this personification of Edwardian convention began the letter with "Dear Efrem," and ended with "Sincerely, Edgar;" and that was the way I addressed him from then on.

In the eight years of our acquaintanceship there was not to be a single event of importance in my life that was not punctuated by a letter from him, or a telegram or phone call. Once, at an affair in the

With FBI director J. Edgar Hoover and General William C. Westmoreland

Enjoying the honor of pinning Skipper's 2nd Lt. bars on at the Pentagon

Pentagon presided over by General William Westmoreland, the Army Chief of Staff who had been my battalion commander in WWII, Edgar Hoover showed up in person. And, on the occasion of Mary Zimbalist's funeral in Philadelphia, as we came out of the church, two agents stepped up to ask if there was anything they could do to be of help. One does not soon forget such kindness.

Nineteen

Among the great lyricists of the twentieth century, surely few can bear comparison to Alan Jay Lerner. There is an inevitability to his words, and to Loewe's music, which makes their songs appear to have been spun from the very warp and woof of our shared experience.

In *My Fair Lady*, Lerner achieved something truly remarkable: a literacy and style the equal of Shaw himself. It is precisely because of this transcendence that two grammatical aberrations strike one as paradoxical. In *Camelot* we hear,

If ever I would leave you, it wouldn't be in springtime.

Crossbreeding the conditional with the subjunctive is commonplace today but from a man of Lerner's attainments, in a song destined never to grow old, is it unreasonable to expect:

"If ever I *should* leave you . . ."?

In someone with a lesser taste for the language the solecism would be accepted with a shrug, but coming from Lerner it is particularly indigestible. The second instance, in *My Fair Lady*, is even more regrettable since it issues from the lips of that embodiment of linguistic rectitude, Professor Higgins himself:

166

I'd be equally as willing for a dentist to be drilling,
Than to ever let a woman in my life.

The parting of the infinitive, albeit without the rod of Moses, is gleefully acceptable but *than* is not. So, finding myself seated across the table from Rex Harrison at a luncheon in Beverly Hills, I saw an opportunity to solve the dilemma once and for all.

"Was it difficult for you," I asked, "to have to sing, 'I'd be equally as willing... *than*?'"

"What in blazes are you talking about?" he snapped.

"I don't know," I replied, feeling the ground slipping away. "I thought, perhaps, *as* would have been more appropriate."

Turning to the person on his right he cried, "Who the devil is this fellow? Some sort of nut?"

Some weeks later I ran into my dear friends, Bobby and Sue Douglas. Knowing they'd find it amusing I told them the story. Bobby wasn't in the least surprised.

"I've known Rex longer than anyone," he explained. "We grew up together in the West End, worked together in the theatre, and came to Hollywood at almost the same time. The fact is, he hardly had any schooling at all, despite his tony accent. He wouldn't know a verb from a turnip!"

Fred MacMurray had one of the sharpest wits in Filmland although, so varied were his gifts, he was not noted for one talent in particular over the others. Some years ago when Fred was in his eighties, we were playing together in a golf tournament in Palm Springs. He took his golf seriously and even at that age was hard to beat, given his handicap.

This was a shotgun tournament, which meant the teams would tee off at the same time on all eighteen holes. As we were waiting by our carts for the signal to proceed to our designated tees, a young man in his late twenties strode up to Fred. Tall, strong and hirsute, with a vibrant energy dismaying to one of Fred's years, he said, in a booming voice as he held out his hand, "Mr. MacMurray, it's a great honor for me to be playing on your team. I've been an admirer of yours since I was a little boy. I've enjoyed everything you've ever done. I hope you'll be patient with me, I'm just beginning."

"I'm just finishing," said Fred.

In the film *Too Much, Too Soon*, Errol Flynn played the role of his idol, John Barrymore, who had tutored him in the fine art of drinking. Errol arrived for work each morning with a quart of vodka which, by lunchtime, was gone. The task of sneaking a second quart past the guard at the Warner Brothers gate fell to his stand-in, Paul McWilliams, who at the end of the picture became my stand-in and remained with me for twenty years. Errol, despite his huge intake of alcohol (two quarts was merely the amount he consumed while at work), never betrayed the least sign of tipsiness. Whatever wreckage he was experiencing on the inside, outwardly he was ever affable and charming.

Too Much, Too Soon, the litany of Diana Barrymore's doings, was directed by a man named Art Napoleon, who with his wife, Josephine (yes, Josephine!), handled the combined chores of producing, writing and directing. Art Napoleon, whose height was identical to that of his famous predecessor, was wont to convey his thoughts while standing skin-close and speaking in decibels barely above a whisper. This presumption of intimacy was annoying beyond words to Errol, who was forever pushing him away.

The real meat of the Barrymore role was a drunken scene toward the end of the picture. Several pages long and highly charged emotionally, it would have been a daunting challenge to any actor, and was to Errol because his memory for lines at this point was markedly eroded. Nonetheless, he sailed through it in a bravura performance on the very first take, eliciting from cast and crew an ovation that must have warmed his heart.

With Errol Flynn in Too Much, Too Soon

The scene would, of course, be accented by closer coverage, but to everyone present this master shot could never be improved on; to everyone, that is, but the little corporal. Before the applause died down he had moved in up against Errol's chest and was cataloging, sotto voce, all the quiddities he imagined might improve the scene.

This was too much for Errol, who thrust him savagely away, pinned him at arm's length and cried, in his best Barrymore manner, "Are you, Art Napoleon, telling ME...how to play a drunk!!!!!"

Stephanie and I were invited to a dinner party one night at the David O. Selznicks. The producer and his wife, Jennifer Jones, were living in a picturesque and secluded house that had been the hideaway of John Gilbert and Greta Garbo.

I have always been a great admirer of Selznick's films and, as I was seated close to him at the table, had a chance to tell him so. I mentioned that, in my opinion, his noble line of pictures was unrivaled in all of Hollywood, an assessment that elicited his thanks.

Referring to *Gone With The Wind*, I continued, "It must be a source of enormous gratification and pride to have produced what is probably the greatest movie ever made."

"That's for others to decide," he replied, "but I can tell you it wasn't easy. We had more than our share of trouble before it was over."

"Casting Gable was inspirational," I went on. "Did Margaret Mitchell write the book with him in mind?"

"No, she didn't and I'm afraid I can't take credit, either, for Clark Gable playing Rhett Butler."

"I don't understand."

"The fact is, I wanted Errol Flynn for the role. Unfortunately, he was under contract to Warner Brothers, who would only lend him out if I agreed to 'borrow' Bette Davis as well, for Scarlett. I didn't think she was right for the part but I wanted him so badly I consented to take her.

"Then they began to get fancy with the figures and during what turned out to be an extended negotiation, letters started pouring in from all over the country saying, 'We want Gable!' As Warner's grew tougher and tougher in their stance tens of thousands of letters flooded our offices, all demanding Gable as Rhett Butler. With Warner Brothers showing no sign of bending I finally offered the part to Clark and the rest is history. I didn't cast him, the public did. I wish I could say it was my idea."

Although I am a votary of both, I confess that trying to visualize Errol Flynn carting Bette Davis up the grand staircase at Tara prompted me to conclude that the Brothers Warner should have been awarded a special Oscar in 1939 . . . for unpremeditated casting services.

I first met Gary Cooper in my own home. Stephanie came to know him and his wife, Rocky, and invited them to dinner. We had bought a house in Beverly Hills which sat on almost an acre and a half of land, with a natural brook that splashed through several fishponds before leaving us for its rendezvous with destiny.

After dinner when Gary expressed a desire to see the property he, one other male guest and I stepped out onto the terrace. As we stood there enjoying the evening he remarked, "You've got a nice piece of land here." These words were spoken as he casually unzipped his fly, and with total unconcern proceeded to sprinkle the weeds while continuing with, "Yes, sir, a real nice piece of land."

I don't know when I've ever received a greater compliment. His action, more eloquent than any words, stated with tribal candor, "I like you and I want to be your friend." It did more: Coming from one who had spent many nights under the stars it pronounced, in the currency of the wild, a benediction upon our new home.

There existed among the great directors during the golden age of Hollywood a curious eroseness, a want of nicety to their work. Things were not neatly wrapped up and tied with a pretty bow. Rough edges were left untended, crucial moments unstressed. One was struck by an unpreparedness similar to that of a child's mind which has not yet, through formal education, been funneled into approved channels.

Much of this attitude, no doubt, harked back to the days of silent films, when these same directors had stood with megaphone in hand, thinking on their feet as they contended with a host of unexpected developments.

One is reminded of Howard Hawks, who dealt pages out daily to a cast who never saw a completed script; or William Wyler who, in filming *Wuthering Heights*, reputedly brought Laurence Olivier and Merle Oberon down a flight of stairs countless times without dialogue, waiting for the take that would strike him as "funny." In numerous scenes during the filming of *The Chapman Report* George Cukor, a most articulate man, would mutter direction larded with four-letter words that was totally incomprehensible to me: I just pretended I knew what he was talking about!

It seemed to me that Gary Cooper, as an actor, embodied these same attitudes. He smiled when there appeared to be no reason, his movements were often jerky, his pauses unaccountable. He heard, as the saying goes, a different drummer.

At a large dinner party given by the Coopers, Stephanie and I were seated at a table outside with Gary and Rocky and the Brian

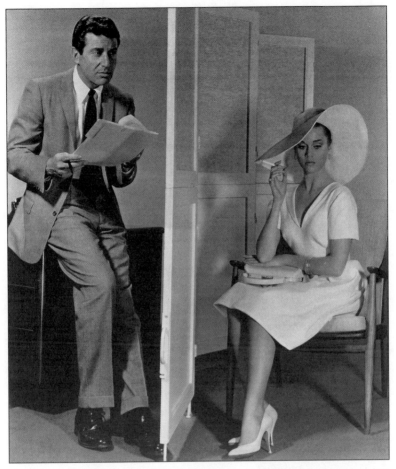

With Jane Fonda in The Chapman Report *(1962)*

Ahernes. When the hour for the cigars to come out and the ladies to go in arrived, the three of us men remained at the table for a half-hour or so; I sat spellbound, listening to their stories and reminiscences. Gary rose at last and Brian Aherne chuckled as he watched him disappear into the house. Noting my questioning look, he said, "Years ago I did a film with that poor son-of-a-bitch. It was one of the most embarrassing times of my life. He was so awkward, so inept, so bumbling that, sitting off camera, we would turn our backs in order not to be part of his mortification. Some months after production there was a screening at the studio and I went to study my work in the picture. I never saw myself. He was so magnetic, I couldn't take my eyes off him."

Close to the end of his life Gary Cooper was given a special Academy Award. He was not in attendance, however, when a tearful Jimmy Stewart made the presentation.

At work the next morning there was speculation that Gary might have cancer, and although I hadn't seen him in some months I thought immediately of Dr. Rosete. Not knowing whether Gary was indeed suffering from the disease or, if he was, whether he was aware of it, I felt I had to proceed cautiously.

I tried all morning to reach his house by telephone but for four hours the line was busy. (I found out later that Rocky had taken the phone off the hook.) I didn't want to intrude on their privacy and yet I felt compelled, should the speculation prove to be true, to offer information that might possibly save his life. With this in mind, at lunchtime I jumped into the Packard, which I had taken to work, and drove out to their house.

As I pulled up he was coming out the front door, supported by his lovely daughter, Maria. Frail as he was and stooped over, he spotted the Packard and made his way over.

"I used to have one just like this," he said, and insisted on climbing into the back seat and sitting down. Despite what the effort must have cost him he went on, patting the leather, "They don't make 'em like this any more."

Sliding out with difficulty, he continued, "We're just off to see the doctor. I have to be back here by three for a press conference. I guess they want to know if I'm going to kick off."

Having thus learned what I needed to, I said, "Gary, I know a wonderful doctor in Mexico who might be able to help you. If you're interested I'd like to tell you about him."

"I sure am," he replied. "When we get back, I'll call you on the set."

"No," I said, "we both know how hard it is to reach someone that way. I'll call you."

After two hours elapsed I tried to phone him but heard the same busy signal; it continued throughout the afternoon. We finished shooting for the day and I felt that, although I might be making a nuisance of myself, I would be less than a friend if I failed to tell him something he clearly wanted to know; there was nothing to do, but drive out to his house a second time.

When I told the maid who opened the door that I wished to speak with Mr. Cooper, she replied that he was in his room and couldn't be disturbed. (I learned afterwards that he never left his bed again.) So I requested to see Mrs. Cooper, but was told she was having a massage.

Almost in desperation I asked, "Is their daughter home?" The maid responded by ushering me into a room, where I was presently joined by Maria.

I jotted down quickly what she would need to know and handed her the slip of paper, saying, "Maria, the doctor I spoke to your father about this afternoon has been a close personal friend of mine for years. He might be able to help him, and the only reason I came back was that your father wanted to hear more about him. This is his number and his address, and if you need me for anything I'm at your service twenty-four hours a day." With that I left.

The next morning I called home from the set every free moment I had, only to be told by Stephanie that she had heard nothing. Finally, towards noon, she reached me to say that Rocky had phoned at last, and had declined our assistance.

Gary died three weeks later. In retrospect it seems unlikely that anything would have helped him. My only sadness has been that the message I had hoped to bring him, one he had hoped to hear, would forever remain unsaid.

Twenty

 AT THE TIME OF MY DISGRACEFUL EXIT FROM YALE, a statute in Connecticut stipulated that minors were not legally responsible for the debts they incurred. Despite this law, my wonderful father went to New Haven after I was gone and, without ever telling me of it, quietly paid off every penny I owed.

I have never met my father's equal. He was the most sublime of artists, yet he had in him none of the ego too often seen in his profession. He was totally and unequivocally dedicated to revealing the deepest fervor of the composer, not to showing off his own skills. He was of all men the most modest, and possessed a wisdom, patience and kindliness evocative of Socrates. We loved each other as deeply as two men could love, but no reference was ever made to it. Only once did I try, awkwardly, to tell him what he meant to me but he stopped me with: "We know that, son. That's understood; there's no need to speak of it."

With the end of the war and the real beginning of my life, he knew how deeply sorry I was for the years I had thrown away. He saw clearly that nothing could possibly be said to me that I had not already said to myself, many times over. Consequently the subject was never broached; it was as though it hadn't existed.

My father

Decades after the Yale episode, following the close of his career when Ormandy had persuaded him to bid adieu by performing the Beethoven with the Philadelphia Orchestra; and following the death of my second mother, Mary, and his resignation as director of the Curtis, my father moved to Reno to live with my sister Maria.

He had always loved the American West. Unfortunately, he had only a few years to enjoy it before being stricken with cancer. Despite his doctor's best efforts, which included months of chemotherapy, his condition worsened to the point where he was given only days—and perhaps hours—to live.

At this moment of crisis I found him lying in his bed at St. Mary's hospital, immobile and remote. He was barely breathing as I held his hand. His eyes had been closed for days; Suddenly they snapped open and he spoke for the first time: "Son, that was a terrible thing you did to me in New Haven." I couldn't believe my ears! This, after almost forty years of silence!

"I know, Daddy," I said. "I'm so terribly sorry. Please forgive me."

His eyes closed again, but from that moment life began returning to his body. With each day his condition improved dramatically and by the end of the week he was discharged from the hospital. He went on to live another ten years, until the age of ninety-five.

As I drove him home from St. Mary's, I asked, "Daddy, do you re-member what you said to me in the hospital?"

"No," he answered, "what?"

Upon hearing what I told him, a little secret smile, part of his elo-quence I knew so well, crept across his face as he confided, "I must have been terribly sick!"

Before we moved to California, "The Rafters" had been the focal point of our lives. Even in the Philadelphia days, Nancy, Skipper and I would hop into the Packard every Friday without fail and head for Connecticut. They would squeal with delight and cry, "Faster, Daddy, faster! Don't let them pass us!" There was even a day when we made the entire trip of some two hundred miles without being passed once.

The place was so special to us! Far from a mere property—a conglomeration of trees, grass, wood, cement and glass—it was a living, throbbing, loving soul: the repository of our finest moments. Skipper was born in the local hospital and baptized at "The Rafters"; Stephanie and I were married there.

It was only after we moved to California that the embrace, like that of many a longtime friendship, began to loosen. The distance was too great, our lives too busy and gradually the house fell into disuse. Nature which, like gravity, is determined to win in the end,

Skipper's christening, "The Rafters," 1947. Left to right: My father; our beloved help, Mimi and Lizzie; Chandler (godfather); minister; Mary Z.; Nurse Mary Green (holding star); and the proud father.

pressed its claim. Flowers withered, paint shriveled, terraces cracked, shingles fell to the ground; our old friend seemed to be dying.

Then one day Marcia, who had just sold her house on Lake Como, called to ask if she could hole up there. I was delighted to have it occupied and told her to go ahead. She more or less camped out in the house. For three years she endured the New England winters and the loneliness of decay. Marcia was an elderly lady by then and unable to fight back; counterattacking is for the young. Finally she departed for California, leaving things worse than when she arrived. Faced with this situation, my father and I were considering the unthinkable . . . consulting a real estate agent.

At this juncture Nancy, who like the rest of us had been living in California, went back to spend a month at "The Rafters." The following year, 1978, she moved to New York and, with her companion Alice O'Leary, began driving up on weekends. They found the overgrowth so pervasive that even the garden beds had disappeared. Each weekend they worked, cleaning, scrubbing, pulling weeds and clearing brush. Nancy hired a part-time gardener and handyman and almost imperceptibly, "The Rafters" began to stir from its long slumber.

As Nancy and Alice made it their home, albeit for weekends only, the house seemed to sense that at last this was no trifling romance. Charlie Anderson's swimming pool had long since become a junkpile of shattered concrete but Nancy installed a brand new pool with a filtration system and slate coping, which the old structure had never had. A new roof replaced the old, rotten shingles on the house and new paint rejuvenated the clapboards outside and the walls within.

Nancy worked tirelessly in the garden, weeding, trimming, fertilizing and planting. Unbelievably, she found some of the old Olmsted peonies and roses were still there. To these she added day lilies, phlox, poppies, coralbells and a host of annuals. As a testament to her achievement, in 1996 the Garden Conservancy, an eminent horticultural society, requested permission for its members to visit "The Rafters" in order to view its garden and grounds.

Daughter Nancy

The cherished place has found its smile again. The guest book groans with the names of family and friends who have spent the weekend, savored Alice's *cordon bleu* cuisine and sensed something unique, an unfamiliar peace. Skipper manages to go there a number of times during the year, as do his four children; Young Stephanie undertook on her own to have the guest cottage rebuilt, and she checks her heart at "The Rafters" every time she leaves. Meanwhile, out of their goodness, she and her brother generously share expenses with Nancy.

On top of the hill, a stone's throw from where Arnold Toynbee sat musing, stands the ancient graveyard, which Daddy used to visit every time he came to "The Rafters." He's there himself now, along with Mother, Mary, Emily, Maria and Marcia. Nearby lie the Carpenters, Dick Ludlam and the Gilkysons, surrounded by three centuries of fellow wayfarers whose stories are yet to be told.

One day when I first came to California, I received a call from Forest Lawn Cemetery.

"Mr. Zimbalist," said a castor-oil voice, "have you made the ultimate preparations?"

"Thank you," I replied, "for being concerned with my final disposition; but the fact is, my family has a plot in a graveyard in Connecticut and I hope to be buried there myself."

"I congratulate you, Mr. Zimbalist," he oozed, "for having the foresight to make these arrangements in advance, but (ahem) there is still the matter of transportation, isn't there?"

Epilogue

 FISHERS ISLAND, WHERE MY EARLY CHILDHOOD summers were spent, is a lovely resort which lies off the coast of Connecticut but is counted part of New York state. The western-most tip of the island was the site of a large coast artillery post, Fort H.G. Wright, since dismantled but constituting at that time, with its mortars and twelve-inch recoiling guns, a major element in the defense of New York Harbor and the Long Island Sound.

Access to the island was (and still is) by ferry from New London and it was possible, if one missed the last departure of the day, to hop on the government boat and arrive at the fort slip. Residents enjoyed an easygoing relationship with the military, because on an island whose length was hardly more than a dozen miles, the interests of both overlapped in many ways.

Our house, a harvest of my beloved parents' genius and hard work, sat in solitary splendor atop a bluff that dominated Hay Harbor, on the fort half of the island. This was a sailing harbor, dotted

Top: The Fishers Island house in the beginning (dock at right)
Middle: The Fishers Island house in its heyday
Bottom: The Fishers Island house today

with skidoos and OneDesigns and the occasional yacht that pulled in for the weekend. The nerve center of all this activity was the modest Hay Harbor Club, which lay on the east shore of the harbor and lent its name to a nine-hole golf course.

As a little boy I was too young to attend the club dances for which my sister Maria, three years my senior, was eligible. Listening to the glamorous stories she brought back, from a world peopled with sophisticated eleven-and twelve-year-olds, filled me with an inchoate longing. From my bed I could hear, across the water, the songs they danced to and dallied to, songs which to this day exert their bittersweet spell upon me. Although I only became aware of it in later years, many of these tunes were identified with Bing Crosby. He was thereby foundational to my childhood.

The only movies on the island were shown in the Service Club at the fort on Saturday afternoons. The army would later build a large theatre, in 1932, but by that time we had left Fishers Island, never to return.

Those were silent movies, in black and white of course, projected on a flickering screen, with frequent breakdowns and re-threadings. Those Saturday events were, nonetheless, the most thrilling of my entire life. It's true I was young and impressionable, but the movies themselves were not much older. There was a freshness and excitement to them impossible to convey to someone who never lived those years. To this day I would rather watch an old silent film than anything that has come since.

In that building my exposure to the silver world of the movies, and especially to Douglas Fairbanks, my greatest hero, began. He wore the crown, but there were many other radiant ones: Buster Keaton, Mary Pickford, Harold Lloyd, Rudolph Valentino, Clara Bow, Charlie Chaplin, Pearl White and Rin Tin Tin.

They were my childhood idols and their lustre has never faded; but the peculiar identity-sharing chimera I sensed, like the blood-mixing in an Indian rite, persevered in certain cases through my youth and into adulthood, all the way to Audrey Hepburn. She was the last. Working with Audrey, the sublimest jewel in Hollywood's tiara, was like floating inside the "Mona Lisa," behind the smile.

With Audrey Hepburn in a scene from Wait Until Dark *(1967)*

These luminaries were the ones who spoke to me in a private language unfamiliar to others, a language arcane and wondrous. By far the most meaningful outcome of my fifty years in Hollywood was catching up with these shimmering raptures from the past, coming full circle, as it were.

I came to know Bing Crosby through the game of golf. We were members of the same club. For seventeen years I played in his precedent-setting tournament in Pebble Beach. In Der Bingle a little boy's longing found consummation at last.

Fairbanks I never knew, (although he once insisted on jumping out of a three-story window for my mother, despite her protestations!). But the connection was preserved by Mary Pickford, who interviewed me at Pickfair in my early days at Warner Brothers for a radio program she was doing at the time. Her subsequent husband, Buddy Rogers, was a golfing pal of mine, as was Dick Arlen, his co-star in *Wings*. That movie introduced, in an unforgettable cameo, a young actor named Gary Cooper.

I had the honor of working with Doris Kenyon, Gloria Swanson and Francis X. Bushman, who was as great a star in his day as any. Clara Bow was a fan of *77 Sunset Strip*, and became a good friend of Stephanie's and mine, although she would not allow herself to be seen, and communicated only by phone and letter.

Over the years I had the privilege of coming to know, and in many cases working with, a large number of those who had shed their light upon my path. In the montage of my memory they all pass in silent black-and-white review before me.

I don't go to the movies any more; I haven't in over twenty years. Still, my estrangement in no way delimits the gratitude I owe those who cast a web of enchantment about a young boy I came to know all over again, in their reflection. I am grateful to each and every one.

I am grateful for the elegance they lent their profession and the perfume that lingered, long after they were gone.

Most of all I am grateful to the dear Lord for His own supercolossal, big-bang, star-studded extravaganza in gorgeous Technicolor, and (as if He didn't have more important things to think about) for finding a tiny walk-on role in it for the likes of me.

Index

A

B

ℳ

Tufts, Sonny, 141
Turner, Lana, 135, 136

U

United States Golf Association, 11, 12

V

Valentino, Rudolph, 186
Vanity Fair, 12
Valentine, Paul, 95
Verdi, Giuseppi, 67

W

Walker, Nancy, 104
Walsh, Raoul, 125
Warner Brothers, 118, 121, 123, 124, 132, 133, 135, 137, 140, 157, 168, 170, 171, 188
Warner, Jack, 119, 123, 126, 130, 147
Warwick Hotel, The, 94, 96
Waterloo Bridge, 126
Watts, Richard, 74, 77
Webb, Jack, 147
Webster, Ben, 61
Webster, Margaret, 61, 63, 64
Welles, Orson, 40
Westmoreland, General William C., 157, 164, 165
Weston, Melissa, 99, 100

ABOUT THE AUTHOR

The son of two legendary parents, soprano Alma Gluck and violinist Efrem Zimbalist, the author began his professional career on Broadway in *The Rugged Path* by Robert E. Sherwood. He went on to appear in four plays with the American Repertory Theatre, followed, the next year, by a role opposite Eva Le Galliene in *Hedda Gabler*.

Zimbalist next tried his hand at producing. With Chandler Cowles and Edith Luytens he presented the twin bill of Gian Carlo Menotti's *The Medium* and *The Telephone*, bringing opera to Broadway audiences for the first time. Three years later he and Cowles presented *The Consul* of Menotti, which won the Pulitzer Prize for 1950.

A contract with Warner Brothers brought the actor to Hollywood, where he appeared in six films during his first year: *Bombers B-52; Band of Angels; The Deep Six; Violent Road; Too Much, Too Soon;* and *Home Before Dark.* In later years he was to add such pictures as *The Crowded Sky, A Fever in the Blood, The Chapman Report, By Love Possessed, Wait Until Dark,* and *Airport '75.* But these were television years for Zimbalist, marked by two series which attained the top rating in the country, *77 Sunset Strip* and *The FBI.*

His many television specials include *Who Is the Black Dahlia?, The Gathering, A Family Upside Down, The Best Place to Be,* and *Scruples,* to name a few. Zimbalist's last screen appearance was in *Hot Shots.*

Zimbalist, the father of Stephanie Zimbalist, lives in Solvang, California.